INSPIRATIONAL GUIDE FOR THE IMPLEMENTATION OF PRME

Second Edition: Learning to Go Beyond

 Principles for Responsible Management Education

 Foundation for the Global Compact

Routledge
Taylor & Francis Group

LONDON AND NEW YORK

PRME Principles for Responsible
Management Education

Foundation for the
Global Compact

First published 2013 by Greenleaf Publishing Ltd

Published 2017 by Routledge
2 Park Square, Milton Park, Abingdon, Oxon OX14 4RN
711 Third Avenue, New York, NY 10017, USA

Routledge is an imprint of the Taylor & Francis Group, an informa business

Cataloguing in Publication data:
   A catalogue record for this book is available from the British Library.

ISBN-13: 978-1-906093-13-6 (pbk)

Contents

Section 2 – Beyond the classroom: Scaling experiential learning 53

Section 3 – Beyond the business school: Mainstreaming PRME across HEIs 89

Section 4 – Beyond campus introspection: Making impact through networks 109

Section 5 – Beyond education-only: Harnessing research and publication 135

Appendices 153

PRME Principles for Responsible
Management Education

Greenleaf Publishing/PRME Book Series –
For Responsibility in Management Education

The Greenleaf Publishing/Principles for Responsible Management Education (PRME) book series aims to highlight the important work of PRME, a United Nations supported initiative. The series will provide tools and inspiration for all those working to make management education fit for purpose in creating a new generation of enlightened leaders for the 21st century.

Acknowledgements

Co-editors:

Merrill Csuri
Oliver Laasch
F. Byron (Ron) Nahser
Giselle Weybrecht

Commissioned by the PRME and CEEMAN Secretariats
Jonas Haertle (Head, PRME Secretariat) and Danica Purg
(President, CEEMAN; 2013 Chair, PRME Steering Committee)

Higher education institutions submitted case stories for the second edition of the Inspirational Guide in response to an open call for contributions to the 2013 PRME Summit – 5th Annual Assembly and were selected through a blind review process. We would like to thank all contributors and reviewers, whose details are listed in Appendix 4.

About PRME

The Principles for Responsible Management Education (PRME) is a United Nations Global Compact sponsored initiative with the mission to inspire and champion responsible management education, research and thought leadership globally. The Six Principles of PRME are inspired by internationally accepted values, such as the Ten Principles of the Global Compact. They seek to establish a process of continuous improvement among institutions of management education in order to develop a new generation of business leaders capable of managing the complex challenges faced by business and society in the 21st century. Currently, over 500 signatories have signed up to PRME, representing 80 countries. PRME's Steering Committee comprises global and specialised associations, including AACSB International (the Association to Advance Collegiate Schools of Business), the European Foundation for Management Development (EFMD), the Association of MBAs (AMBA), the Graduate Management Admission Council (GMAC), the Association of African Business Schools (AABS), the Association of Asia–Pacific Business Schools (AAPBS), CEEMAN (formerly Central and East European Management Development Association), CLADEA (the Latin American Council of Management Schools), ABIS (The Academy of Business in Society, formerly EABIS), and the Globally

Responsible Leadership Initiative (GRLI). For more information, please visit www.unprme.org.

The Six Principles of PRME and the Ten Principles of the Global Compact can be viewed in full in Appendices 1 and 2.

How to use the Guide

Over 500 signatory institutions from around the world are working to transform the way they train the next generation of leaders and managers using the Principles for Responsible Management Education (PRME), both as a framework derived from universally accepted sustainability principles and as part of a dynamic learning community. The ways in which they choose to do this are unique to each institution, and the Inspirational Guide project is an encouraging example of all of the different ways that responsible management can be embedded into the purpose and values of higher education institutions (HEIs) as well as the way that they teach students, conduct research, and interact with stakeholders. At the same time, challenges faced in mainstreaming sustainability principles remain for all HEIs, regardless of how long they have been signatory to PRME, the size of their institution, or where they are located in the world.

Before reading any single case, it is important to remember that:

- **All of the Six Principles are interrelated and often inseparable:** This is exemplified by the fact that each case story covers more than one. For example, a research project (Principle 4) focused on responsible leadership (Principles 2) started because of involvement with PRME (Principle 1), involved a partnership with a local company (Principle 5), and resulted in a conference that aims to educate both students (Principle 3) and the business community about the outcomes (Principle 6).
- **It does not matter whether you are just starting out or have been a signatory for many years:** The range of case stories offers insights and lessons learnt for implementers of all levels.
- **It does not matter where the institution is located or how big it is:** Examples presented can easily be shaped and moulded to fit your own institution, resources, and focus areas.
- Many of the highlighted projects were put in place using limited resources, either in terms of staff or money, or both. **Often, all you need is a group of committed individuals to champion these efforts and get things started.**

What is in each case story?

The case stories focus on a particular programme, project, or activity that an institution has implemented around responsible management. Each short case story contains:

- An **introduction** to the contributing institution and the story highlighted
- An overview of the particular **challenge(s) faced** in relation to mainstreaming responsible management
- An explanation of the **actions taken** in relation to the challenge(s) outlined

- Information about the **results** and/or **benefits** of the actions taken
- Some points regarding **the role of PRME/sustainability principles** in helping to inspire and/or carry out the activity

The following case stories can be used as a source of:

- **New ideas and inspiration for how you can implement sustainability principles on your campus:** The case stories cover a wide range of different ways to embed responsible management into teaching, research, partnerships, and the culture of an institution, many of which are quite innovative.
- **Advice for schools thinking of implementing something similar:** You may already have decided that you want to create a similar programme, and seeing how other signatories have approached their respective initiatives may help to structure your thinking and next steps.
- **Inspiration on how to further your current efforts:** You may already be undertaking a similar activity on campus, and seeing how other institutions have implemented their projects can help you to further develop or scale efforts up.

What topics are covered?

The case stories cover a wide range of topics relevant both to new signatories that are just starting out and to schools with more established programmes. This includes, but is not limited to:

- How to get started
- How to embed responsible management into:
  - Institutional culture
  - Curriculum
  - Research and publications

- How to create and work with networks and partnerships
- How to evaluate progress and report on achievements

Want more information about what PRME signatories are doing?

The PRME community offers many different ways to share case stories and learn from others, including:

- The Inspirational Guide project
- Sharing Information on Progress (SIP) reports
- The *PRiMEtime* blog
- PRME Annual Assemblies
- PRME Regional Chapters and Meetings
- Working Group activities and PRME projects
- Share your story via social media. You can engage with PRME on Twitter, Facebook, and LinkedIn.
- Reach out to PRMESecretariat@unrpme.org or to fellow signatories directly

Introduction

Where we came from

Since the inception of the **United Nations Global Compact** sponsored initiative **Principles for Responsible Management Education** (PRME) in 2007, there has been increased debate over how to adapt management education to best meet the demands of the 21st century. While consensus has been reached by the majority of globally focused management education institutions that sustainability[1] must be incorporated into management education, the relevant question is no longer why management education should change, but **how**?

Making the Principles of PRME (Appendix 1) central to management education and academic activities requires time and commitment in order to embed this new set of values (Principle 2), experiment with new and more impactful educational frameworks (Principle 3), undertake conceptual and empirical research (Principle 4), engage with and learn from managers (Principle 5), and establish a constant dialogue with stakeholders (Principle 6),

---

[1] Across the PRME community, different concepts are used; most frequent are corporate (social) responsibility, responsible leadership, and sustainable value creation for business and society.

which results in a sustainability-oriented business view that references the Ten Principles of the Global Compact (Appendix 2) and penetrates through to the broader society (Principle 1).

Progressive and promising work is under way, and innovative solutions are already being implemented by the more than 500 PRME signatories that represent a truly global spread of many of the most advanced and consolidated management schools and higher education institutions (HEIs), globally. The PRME initiative offers both a framework for change and platform for continuous learning for implementers of responsible management education through adoption of the Six Principles, a reporting framework for HEIs (Sharing Information on Progress (SIP) reports), engagement in PRME Working Groups and projects, and participation in regional and global meetings, such as the PRME Global Fora and Summits.

Although the PRME initiative is set to increase to 1,000 signatories by 2015, it is equally important for the PRME community to cultivate actively engaged participants. While the Principles provide a guiding framework, practical implementation varies greatly across regions and programmes. In order to inspire signatories to go further, published in 2012, the *Inspirational Guide for the Implementation of PRME: Placing Sustainability at the Heart of Management Education* sought to inspire further integration of PRME by highlighting real world examples of the Principles in practice.

Given the positive reception and impact of the first Guide, members of the PRME community requested that a second edition of the Guide be compiled for the 2013 PRME Summit – 5th Annual Assembly, hosted by PRME Steering Committee member CEEMAN in Bled, Slovenia, 25–26 September. Through an open call and blind review process, 27 (of 63) cases were selected, representing 25 institutions from 17 countries.

This second edition highlights the real implementers of responsible management education, and their stories are truly inspirational. The evolving picture underscores the important changes already taking place, the role of PRME in effecting such change, and also that continuous experimenting, innovating, and learning is required to go beyond initial constructs of both management education and sustainability.

Learning to go beyond

Although each individual case presents a unique path of progress and learning, several key strategic dimensions are found throughout. When reviewing cases for this second edition, it was clear that there has been a qualitative shift in implementation. Most of the cases not only built on, but also went beyond the leading practices in the first edition. The subtitle of this Guide, 'Learning to Go Beyond', makes reference to this exciting development, while highlighting the continuous implementation and learning processes that are necessary not only to keep up with 21st-century sustainability concerns, but also to go beyond.

The five sections of this Guide reflect the theme of 'learning to go beyond', both in critical areas of practice and in current trends in responsible management education, including:

1. Beyond knowledge-only: Creating new competences
2. Beyond the classroom: Scaling experiential learning
3. Beyond the business school: Mainstreaming PRME across HEIs
4. Beyond campus introspection: Making an impact through networks
5. Beyond education-only: Harnessing research and publication

Figure 1 further illustrates how the five trends are organised, from 'small to big' and 'specific to broad'. Highlighting these trends should not distract us from the crucial importance of the Principles in creating practices that go beyond. We can observe a similar development in the established domains of sustainability, responsibility, and ethics, which are increasingly used together, highlighting their complementary contributions to management education. As you will see, in most of the cases, it is the creative combination of several of the Principles that enables PRME signatories to go beyond.

FIGURE 1 **Five trends of 'learning to go beyond' in responsible management education**

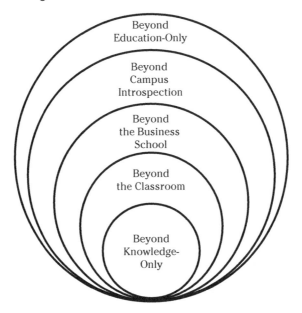

Beyond
Education-Only

Beyond
Campus
Introspection

Beyond
the Business
School

Beyond
the Classroom

Beyond
Knowledge-
Only

1. Beyond knowledge-only: Creating new competences

Any educational endeavour starts with uncovering the competencies that we want to form among our students. What competencies does a responsible manager need? Many signatory institutions are excellent at educating students about sustainability, responsibility, and ethics, but is the attainment of knowledge sufficient? There is more about a responsible manager than pure domain competencies (to know). Self-competencies (to be/to think/to learn), social competencies (to interact), and procedural competences (to do) for responsible management are equally important. The cases in this section highlight how to go beyond transmitting knowledge towards transforming people.

In this section, learn from:

- Copenhagen Business School's 'Responsibility Day', where more than 2,700 incoming bachelor students are aided in creating awareness for the importance of responsibility in business 'from day one'
- Aalto University School of Business about how to help students form a systemic vision of responsible management, integrated throughout all functions of a business
- The University of Notre Dame Mendoza College of Business, which facilitates the development of critical, creative, and systems thinking skills by confronting students with global challenges and their immediate business repercussions
- The University of Washington Tacoma Milgard School of Business helps students build leadership skills through a mix between internship and classroom interaction
- Nottingham University Business School's efforts to further social, emotional, and spiritual intelligence by facilitating students' immersion into the 'social, cultural, political, and moral complexity' of leadership
- Babson College, where MBA students and their instructor embark on a journey of self-discovery to 'The land of cheese and wine'
- The University of Auckland, which teaches students to learn to *be responsible* instead of simply learning 'about' responsibility through experiential exercises that foster moral intuition, observation, and emotion
- The University of Auckland Business School and ESPOL-ESPAE Graduate School of Management how the focus on teamwork among students and professors creates competencies for responsible management

Copenhagen Business School's 'Responsibility Day':

'This case presents a powerful idea that will be useful to all PRME signatories in thinking about how to introduce PRME commitments early to students while also indicating institutional commitment to PRME to faculty, who may then be more motivated to engage with the Principles in other areas of their work (curriculum, research, partnerships).'
Elizabeth Goldberg, Babson College

2. Beyond the classroom: Scaling experiential learning

The classroom is a great place for conceptual knowledge, but it is limited in its richness of experiences. Experiential learning, learning through experience, is an umbrella for a variety of powerful educational method for creating the very competencies noted in the first section. There are a colourful bunch of experiential practices that include, for instance, service learning, action learning, social learning, immersions, and project-based learning.

In this section, learn from:

- Leeds University Business School, which helps students to develop new values and change their attitudes by meeting 'the farmers behind the coffee'
- The University of the West of England Faculty of Business and Law put sustainability 'in-context' in the Danube Parks
- Bentley University's Center for Service Learning, which enables students to gain credits by running a social enterprise
- Rotterdam School of Management at Erasmus University offers a course on 'Companies in Ecologies,' which is taught at a botanic garden
- The American University in Cairo (AUC) Corporate Governance Club, where students learn through competitions and games
- The Externado University of Colombia, where executives directly apply responsible management at their jobs
- Lagos Business School, which brings the action into the classroom through creative use of media

3. Beyond the business school: Mainstreaming PRME across HEIs

The interdisciplinary nature and transcendent importance of sustainability, responsibility, and ethics calls for coverage of these topics in many areas that go beyond the business school and lead to action that embeds PRME in an interdisciplinary and larger institutional context.

In this section, learn from:

- Aston University's efforts to expand the work of the Business School to other disciplines and to ensure that all organisational practices serve as examples to their students by developing a university-wide ethical framework
- Coventry University Faculty of Business, Environment and Society on how to create a faculty-wide vision of sustainability and how to apply it on courses from topic areas as different as geology, languages, sociology, and law
- ESADE's high-level leadership fosters 'progress in order to create an increasingly socially responsible academic institution'

4. Beyond campus introspection: Making impact through networks

Responsible management education works 'better together' is the underlying mantra of this section, in which the cases show how academic institutions work in greater networks to scale their impact.

In this section, learn from:

- The IEDC-Bled School of Management engages with the Global Compact Network Slovenia to make a bigger impact for integrity and sustainability
- IAE Business School facilitated transformation in a whole economic sector
- Ivey Business School at Western University developed a partnership with business schools in 32 African countries to enable them to better assume their roles as change agents for sustainable development
- Sabanci University School of Management teamed up with an executive search firm and the Swedish consulate in Istanbul to impact gender equality in corporate boards
- ISAE engages with multiple actors to empower responsible management education in Brazil

5. Beyond education-only: Harnessing research and publication

PRME is an educational initiative, so it is not further surprising that most of the efforts covered in the Guide are educational efforts. In this last section, we want to focus on the 'sweet spot', where education and research go hand in hand and are immediately, mutually reinforcing.

Glasgow Caledonian University

'This case is firmly inspirational in terms of research and demonstrates an institutional commitment to engaging in research on 'big' societal challenges.'
Kathryn Haynes,
Newcastle University
Business School

In this section, learn from:

- Glasgow Caledonian University, where students simultaneously hone their research skills and learn about social issues, and staff of the Yunus Centre for Social Business and Health co-create social impact and research
- The Center for Responsible Management Education creates educational materials for responsible management education through textbook publishing

Section 1

Beyond knowledge-only
Creating new competencies

1 Responsibility Day: A tool for setting expectations of incoming first-year bachelor students

Copenhagen Business School

Copenhagen, Denmark

Introduction

Each year about 2,700 new students start their first semester in one of 18 bachelor programmes at Copenhagen Business School (CBS). The students' first day on campus, Responsibility Day, is dedicated to the topic of responsible management. The aim of the day is to provide students with an opportunity to reflect on social responsibility and ethical dilemmas, both in their new role as CBS students and in their future role as business managers. Furthermore, the aim is to set expectations for what role responsible management education should and will play in their upcoming years of study.

Faculty from each study programme are teaching on Responsibility Day, and as a result are engaged in developing the learning environment of the actual day. However, more important is the way in which the initiative impacts the general educational framework of responsible management by kick-starting curriculum development and facilitating the signalling of CBS's values. Hence, by developing a learning environment for responsible management education in each study programme from the very first day, Responsibility Day creates extensive impact across CBS.

Challenges

When students attend business school they usually expect core courses, such as marketing and economics, to form the main part of their education. At CBS we want to signal our dedication to responsible management on the students' very first day of lectures, as well as set students' expectations for how their future study programmes will deliver responsible management education. In order to prove the relevance and strategic substance of responsible management education to individual bachelor programmes, we needed a way to perceptibly demonstrate the implementation of PRME and engage faculty and study programmes across the board at CBS. One approach for attaining these objectives was set in motion by the Dean of Education at CBS with the launch of Responsibility Day – on the first day of lectures for all incoming bachelor students CBS makes its commitment to responsible management education explicitly across all study programmes.

Actions taken

Responsibility Day starts with morning sessions where the students of each study programme, varying in number from 60 to 650 students, discuss a relevant case of responsible management together with a senior faculty member. In 2013 the case will focus on the philanthropic projects and supply chain of the iconic Danish apparel company, Hummel. In the afternoon sessions, the students are assembled and welcomed to CBS by senior management, which is followed by real-life examples of responsible management presented by keynote speaker, Christian Stadil, creative director and owner of the case company, Hummel.

On Responsibility Day, the students have the opportunity to start working with the case supported by a designated instructor, after which they have three weeks to finish a case solution for submission. A jury will select the three best-case solutions to be pitched during Green Week, when the winning group will be announced. During Green Week, CBS promotes sustainability to both students and faculty through company presentations, events, and student activities. By extending Responsibility Day into Green Week, CBS signals that commitment to responsible management is an integral element of our values and education.

Responsibility Day was launched in 2009 and is continuously being developed. In order to evaluate and improve Responsibility Day, a survey is given to students and instructors directly after the event. Study programmes differ significantly in size and nature, requiring, therefore, a high degree of coordination, logistical overview and engagement from our intro teams and programme coordinators. Such challenges are addressed and facilitated by formulation of the Responsibility Day Road Map in which experiences from the preparation and execution of the event are retained and updated each year.

Results and benefits

Responsibility Day aims to illustrate the concept of responsible management and how it relates to each study programme. Students learn to reflect on social responsibility, ethical dilemmas and the like, both in their new role as students as well as in their future careers. In 2012 we conducted six focus group interviews with students who had participated in one of the previous Responsibility Days. Along with feedback from faculty who participated in the event, these interviews indicated that both students and instructors viewed Responsibility Day as an initiative that gives an important foundation and frame of reference for the coming years of studying. Furthermore, it was evident that students clearly remembered Responsibility Day as their first day of lectures.

Moreover, Responsibility Day works as a catalyst for curriculum development. By engaging faculty in Responsibility Day, the initiative creates ownership and encourages study programme directors, instructors, and study board members to focus on responsible management throughout the bachelor programme. Hence, when approaching study programmes concerning PRME initiatives, such as curriculum development or faculty training, faculty are predisposed towards responsible management education and know how it is linked to their individual study programmes.

The role of PRME/sustainability principles

- Responsibility Day is CBS's most important mechanism to signal the commitment to PRME to students and faculty. As it is the first day of lectures, every study programme and student alike are exposed to responsible management education.
- In terms of resources needed, Responsibility Day has proven to be an impactful way of reaching every new bachelor student at CBS.
- Responsibility Day serves as a catalyst for development and implementation of other PRME activities, for example, curriculum development.
- Responsibility Day enables the establishment of synergies and coherence by engaging CBS organisations and initiatives, such as oikos Copenhagen and CBS Goes Green, as well as the teams responsible for the bachelor students' general introduction to CBS.

2 *Improvement of 'sustainability literacy' of first-year business students through innovative business partnerships*

Aalto University School of Business
Helsinki, Finland

Introduction

We approach sustainability-related education through two lenses at the Aalto University School of Business. On the one hand, we train sustainability specialists in our master's programmes Management and Creative Sustainability. On the other hand, we aim at improving the 'sustainability literacy' of all business students, because the lack of knowledge of other managers in companies is one of the major challenges of present-day corporate responsibility officers in business. The latter is the main target of this case story, where we present new developments of first-year business studies at Aalto University School of Business.

Challenges

The corporate responsibility officers of large companies still face the challenge that their fellow managers have too little understanding of sustainability for efficient cooperation in the improvement of company performance. Even though we have offered a fair number of good-quality courses in corporate responsibility at our university, the integration of responsibility issues in the whole curriculum has been insufficient. As a result, many students have failed to understand the importance of corporate responsibility as well as how responsibility issues are related to other management subjects. This has led to rather low motivation towards the topic altogether.

Actions taken

Given the challenges discussed above, sustainability and corporate responsibility have been given more weight and impact in the new degree regulations that will come into effect in academic year 2013–14. Specifically, there will be four major changes:

First of all, the overall learning outcomes of the bachelor programme have been renewed. In the new learning outcomes, sustainability and responsibility issues play an important role; one of the five degree-programme learning outcomes states that when graduating, students are able to analyse business issues from the perspective of ethics, sustainability, and internationality. More specifically, this means that students can identify and analyse questions in their own area of expertise from ethical, social, economic, environmental, and international viewpoints. Including responsibility issues in the overall learning outcomes is hoped to encourage all instructors to bring these issues up in their own courses.

Second, the new degree regulations mean that there will be an introductory course on corporate responsibility and business ethics during the first year of studies. Until now, we have only offered a course in business ethics, which according to student feedback has not been seen as very motivating. The purpose of this change is to broaden the scope of the course so that it better integrates issues discussed in other courses.

The third change is closely related to the second one. We have recruited a specialist whose main responsibility is to ensure the alignment of courses and learning during the first year. This means encouraging the instructors of first-year basic business courses to work together in planning teaching content and methods. In the case of corporate responsibility teaching, this means that there is a dialogue between the responsibility-related issues taught in accounting, financing, marketing, business law, etc. In all basic courses that are taught during the first year, responsibility issues are brought up and discussed whenever appropriate. The specific corporate responsibility course, which is offered in the last period during the first year, will then build on the issues already discussed during other basic courses, referring back to the examples used earlier during the year. Through this dialogue, we aim at helping the students to really understand how responsibility issues are integrated in all business.

Finally, we will introduce two new 1 credit (ECTS) courses to the first-year curriculum, Real Case 1 and Real Case 2. The former takes place already during the students' orientation week before they start studying, and includes an introduction of a case company as well as an introductory session of the different majors offered at the School of Business. The purpose is to give students an understanding of different functions in organisations and help them understand questions related to them in business activities. Real Case 2 takes place at the end of the first year. During that course, the students need to integrate the knowledge and skills they have learned during the first year to solve a real business case presented by another case organisation. In both these courses, corporate responsibility is included as a subject among others, and students need to address responsibility issues in both cases.

Results and benefits

We expect the above discussed changes to benefit our students and teaching staff in three main ways. First, we expect students to gain a strong overall understanding of the role and importance of corporate responsibility and sustainability issues in business, because this understanding will be built course by course. Second, we expect the students to become more motivated to consider responsibility in their own and businesses' behaviour, as they can see that every subject area has critical responsibility issues that might significantly harm business performance if not considered properly. Finally, through encouraging interaction between the instructors of first-year basic business courses, we expect the instructors to become more interested in providing students with a broader perspective to business studies – a perspective that includes corporate responsibility issues at its core.

The role of PRME/sustainability principles

- Development of capabilities (Principle 1)
- Improvement of incorporation of corporate responsibility (Principle 2)
- Improved educational frameworks (Principle 3)

3 *Addressing global challenges with actionable foresight*

Mendoza College of Business University of Notre Dame

Notre Dame, Indiana, United States

Introduction

Mendoza College of Business at the University of Notre Dame is a premier Catholic business school that seeks to foster academic excellence, professional effectiveness, and personal accountability in a context that strives to be faithful to the ideals of community, human development and individual integrity.

In January 2008, Mendoza College of Business became signatory to PRME. In doing so, it joined business schools and academic associations worldwide in committing to align its mission and strategy, as well as its core competencies – education, research, and thought leadership – with UN values embodied by the Six Principles of PRME.

Mendoza continues in its concerted efforts to create measureable progress towards the fulfilment of these Principles, including Principle 3 to create educational frameworks, materials, processes, and environments that enable effective learning experiences for responsible leadership. At Mendoza, research opportunities are vital to gaining a deeper understanding of the power of business and its impact on the environment and the human community. This case story shares one example of these efforts, through the realisation of an undergraduate course called Foresight in Business and Society.

Foresight in Business and Society is a signature course required for all undergraduate business majors. Each academic year since Fall 2009, 500–700 students are challenged to identify and evaluate major issues, trends and uncertainties impacting business and society, and to explore potential business opportunities that can drive sustainable innovation.

The course provides students with a framework, based on foresight skills, for thinking critically about change and decisions regarding the future. It exposes students to quantitative and qualitative methodologies to identify trends, to consider the implications of change, to plan for alternative futures, and to suggest strategies leading to preferred futures. Foresight challenges students to demonstrate critical, creative, and systems thinking skills in order to fully understand complex change and how business can drive positive outcomes across all stakeholder groups. The students apply these thinking skills and the foresight framework in a semester-long team project on a topic of their choosing that combines a significant issue facing the world today with business implications and opportunities in light of moral and ethical concerns. Past projects have addressed a wide variety of topics including health, water, food, energy, education, and sustainability related issues around the world. At the end of the semester, the student teams present their projects at a public presentation using a variety of multimedia options.

Since the team projects involve areas of business where change is imminent, likely to be disruptive, and evolving in real time, there is tremendous opportunity for students to learn from professionals currently working in these areas. Student teams are, therefore, given the opportunity to work with corporate executive mentors that can offer their experience and knowledge throughout the project creation process. Past and current corporate mentors include IBM, GE, Rocky Mountain Institute, Interface Carpet, Dean's Beans, and Changing Our World Inc.

As a result of this course and immersion in their team project, students emerge with a better understanding of how business is addressing global trends and issues, and how they, as future business leaders, can utilise the power of business for societal good.

Challenges

Foresight is a project-based course that is both time and research intensive. The primary challenge for delivering this course is the pace at which teams must proceed through the various stages of the foresight process. The challenge encompasses both in-class design and the design of the project development process. It is critical that students 'buy in' to the value of the process, have access to the information and evidence that they will need to develop their research, and receive timely constructive feedback to guide their progress. Given the tight time constraints of a 16-week semester, it has been the major challenge in developing and refining this innovative pedagogy.

Actions and results

Two deliberate courses of action were particularly successful in addressing this challenge. The first course of action was linking information and foresight skills that are taught in the classroom with their practical application and use in the students' semester projects. This linkage was achieved by aligning team project assignments with information and the same skills and methods that are being taught in the classroom. Through this alignment and by intentionally setting aside class time at critical points in the project development process for student teams to work on their projects in alternative learning environments outside the traditional classroom, the foresight projects are more fully integrated into the course.

The second course of action was to engage the support of business leaders and alumni in emphasising that foresight methods and skills taught in class were essential in an increasingly complex and uncertain world, and ones they looked for in professionals joining their organisations. The use and value of the foresight process in addressing complex global challenges was enforced further through the mentoring programme offered to teams as part of their project experience. Early in the process, teams have the opportunity to submit a proposal to work with one of the many corporate and individual mentors that offer their time and expertise to work with a student team. As they work together, students see first hand that professionals are using foresight methods and skills they are learning in the classroom.

As a result, the students' assessment of the course has continuously improved. It enjoys a level of acceptance that is truly unique for such a challenging course that is required for such a large number of business students regardless of their field of concentration.

For more information about the course and the students' projects, please visit the course website at http://bizcourse.nd.edu/foresight.

The role of PRME/sustainability principles

- Providing focus to the introduction of global issues and how business can be part of the solution to these issues through the context of global social responsibility and sustainable innovation
- Providing a common vision for those at Mendoza involved in this course and their business and alumni partners as they work together in the mentorship programme component of this course

- Providing credibility to Mendoza as a signatory institution of PRME; business partners and alumni understand the commitment that Mendoza makes when allying itself with the PRME initiative and its Principles to deliver on our mission, 'Ask More of Business'

4

Teaching responsible leadership in theory and practice

Milgard School of Business University of Washington Tacoma

Tacoma, Washington, United States

Introduction

A focus on Principle 3 of PRME led the Milgard School of Business at the University of Washington to a curriculum innovation that has proven effective in impacting our students' understanding of responsible leadership and the role of governance in leading organisations to be more effective, more sustainable, and better citizens. The course, Board Governance, is taught through a service-learning internship with local non-profit boards combined with a traditional classroom curriculum that introduces the principles and theory of good governance. This course is a senior-level undergraduate course at the Milgard School of Business. We do have a few graduate students who take the course each year. We currently co-teach the course and spend a fair amount of time recruiting agencies to serve as host boards for our students. We are able to accomplish this due to our Center for Leadership and Social Responsibility, which provides support.

Challenges

The genesis for our course on Board Governance was in the different perspectives that two faculty members brought to conversations about how to better connect students to community in ways that create value for both sides. One faculty member has a background in the non-profit sector, bringing awareness of the demographic limitations of many non-profit boards: members tend to be older, wealthier, and less culturally diverse than the communities being served. The other faculty member's experience in the academic world indicated that students were often not aware of board service, though it is a common role for business and community leaders, and were unlikely to gain a rich understanding of governance without a guided academic experience.

Actions taken

From these perspectives, we developed the idea of an extended undergraduate learning experience that would link students to non-profit boards and leverage both experiential and classroom learning. The students would gain knowledge of governance as well as an understanding of many elements required to manage an organisation: strategic planning, financial oversight, leadership, teamwork, assessment, and guiding change. Students would also develop a valuable set of skills in making sense of new situations, participating in meetings, communicating effectively, making group decisions, and recognising ethical dilemmas. Finally, students would leverage their academic skills to provide their host organisations with research and reflective analysis that could be used to enhance board functioning and governance.

Our extensive search for a course model found examples of student internships at non-profits, courses on governance, and graduate-level board internships, but nothing like the course we had in mind. We decided to build our own course that was tailored to our community, but designed so that it could be replicated by others.

Recognising that we would need support in finding non-profit boards where we could place students, we developed a partnership with a local agency that served as a resource hub for non-profit education, support, and capacity building. At the same time, we worked with an undergraduate student on a research project to identify the academic literature that would underpin a course in non-profit board governance.

We launched the Non-profit Governance course sequence in 2009. The course is now titled Board Governance to emphasise the applicability of governance principles to many contexts. Students begin in Winter quarter with a 2-credit class (the University of Washington system is a quarter system where a 5-credit-hour class is equal to one full class and a full-load is 15 credits) that is designed to introduce them to basic governance principles and immerse them in board service. Students attend board meetings, collect information on the organisation and its governance and present their organisation to their classmates. In Spring quarter, with some organisational knowledge and experience, students take a 5-credit course that extensively explores governance theory and practices, using examples from non-profit, corporate, and government settings. Students continue their board service and engagement with their non-profit until the course concludes in June. They conduct research on a governance topic relevant to their board and produce a written report that is presented to both the professor and the organisation. Although it is not a requirement of the course, a majority of students are invited to make a formal presentation to their boards and provide insights and advice.

Results and benefits

Students not only gain the course knowledge and skills described above, but share their experiences with classmates. They gain greater awareness of the needs of the broader community and the challenges of serving those needs. Students build relationships with board members who serve as role models of citizenship and community service, and gain access to new networks of community members. They also learn a great deal about the 'hidden' aspects of organisational life that are so important to accomplishing goals, such as values, interpersonal and group politics, and building relationships. Finally, students learn extensively from each other and from the variety of approaches to governance taken by different organisations in the community. We believe this is an excellent model for lifelong learning, where insights are gained from many places and 'right' answers may not exist.

Non-profit boards gain another perspective from student apprentices, who are often different from the board members on several dimensions of diversity, ranging from age and ethnicity to values and orientation towards technology. The presence of the student in their meetings encourages them to examine their practices and challenge some of their taken-for-granted assumptions. Some boards gain in a very practical way from the students' work by improving their record-keeping, board member orientation, and communication practices. All the organisations benefit from the opportunity to reflect on governance and to consider students' suggestions for how to better achieve goals. Finally, the boards have access to students as future volunteers, advocates, or permanent board members.

The community as a whole gains from a growing pool of our graduates who both understand the value of service to the non-profit community and have knowledge and skills that are beneficial to boards and organisations. While many boards have sought to increase the diversity of their membership, they are not always well-connected to other segments of the community. Our diverse student population provides an excellent point of access into many sectors of the community, and the students are often willing and able ambassadors.

If you are interested in replicating this model, we have ideas about how you could partner with your community to create the capacity for these board partnerships. For more detailed information on this course series and how it is run, visit the course website at: http://www.tacoma.uw.edu/clsr/board-governance.

The role of PRME/sustainability principles

- Principle 1 – Purpose: This course develops the capabilities of future generators of sustainable value by engaging them in the theory and practice of good organisational governance
- Principle 3 – Method: This course is unique in its delivery and service-learning model
- Principle 5 – Partnership: We partner with leaders of non-profit organisations, a significant sector in the United States, and leaders of environmental and social change

5

The spirit of leadership: New directions in leadership education

Nottingham University Business School

Nottingham, England, United Kingdom

Introduction

Nottingham University Business School (NUBS) has campuses in the United Kingdom, China, and Malaysia and is among a select group of Association of MBAs (AMBA) and EFMD Quality Improvement System (EQUIS) accredited business schools. The School has global reach and a reputation as a leading research institution offering undergraduate, master's, MBA, executive MBA, PhD, and executive education programmes. In particular, NUBS has achieved high standing in business ethics and sustainability research and education over the last decade. The School continues to pursue the goal of embedding sustainability within educational offerings and scholarly activities. This case focuses on one strand of work that challenges traditions of leadership in business and management and proposes an alternative theoretical and pedagogical approach to leadership education.

Challenges

In the latter part of the 20th century the number of students enrolling at business schools grew dramatically, and critics started to raise concerns about the role of business schools as a social institution (Hambrick 1993; Starkey, Hatchuel, and Tempest 2004; Mintzberg 2004). Criticism was levied at the dominance of economic perspectives in business schools, the preoccupation with a narrow set of business values, and excessive attention to developing technical competence at the expense of the human dimensions that shape individuals and organisations. But the voice of a small number of agents provocateurs was all too easy to ignore until the financial crisis of 2008, which amply demonstrated the shortcomings of this approach and spawned global initiatives, including high-profile examples, such as PRME, to challenge the status quo. The challenge of shaping business schools into social institutions that more positively impact society concerns all subject areas, but there is a particular role for leadership research and education to meet the urgent demand for developing future leaders that can contribute to a sustainable global society. Yet the unbalanced economic mind-set of business schools has dominated thinking on leadership, and education programmes, especially MBAs, have focused students too much on a narrowly defined economic bottom line.

Actions taken

NUBS Professor Ken Starkey, who has long been engaged in the debate on business schools' contribution to society, is addressing this problem in collaboration with Professor of Human Relations, Carol Hall. Pursuing forms of business and leadership that are more generative, transcultural, ethical, and sustainable, Starkey and Hall challenge the 'economic narrative' of management and leadership education and, instead, propose a 'social narrative of leadership' that acknowledges the human dimension with all of its social, cultural, political, and moral complexity. They have developed an intercultural perspective on and a teaching practice of leadership that combines insights from a range of the social sciences and humanities – particularly sociology, psychology, education, and philosophy – drawing on theory and practice, both Eastern and Western. Grounded in critical realism, this approach emphasises critical reflection on personal, organisational, and cultural narratives. The pedagogical approach is primarily experiential (Kolb 1984). In supporting the development of social (Goleman 2006), emotional (Mayer and Salovey 1993), and spiritual intelligence (Zohar and Marshall 2000), alongside and in balance with intellectual functioning, it gives weight to the emotional component of the reflection cycle, using structured exercises to facilitate personal exploration of thoughts and feelings, which have their roots in cultural narratives.

This approach to leadership education has been integrated into NUBS' master's and MBA programmes and runs as an executive education module. MBA modules are run over intensive blocks in order to maximise learning and capitalise on the group process. When offered to executive education clients, NUBS recommends a three-day course segmented in the following way: a two-day workshop typically comprising a balance of case study, experiential exercises, tutor input, and personal reflection, followed by an opportunity to apply what has been learned in the clients' own work environment. Blended learning is used such that classroom learning is supported by meetings as learning sets using the web to link members across the globe. The course leaders provide on-going mentoring/coaching. Finally, the group reconvenes to focus on personal and organisational learning from the course and to think through next steps in developing a more balanced philosophy and practice of leadership for the future and what further work needs to be done individually and organisationally. Starkey and Hall's work on leadership education, and their model of 'leadership as a balancing act' (Figure 1) has been published as an essay in the *Handbook for Teaching Leadership* (Snook, Nohria, and Khurana 2012), which captured the output of a Harvard-led initiative on the challenges of educating global leaders.

FIGURE 1 **Leadership as a balancing act**

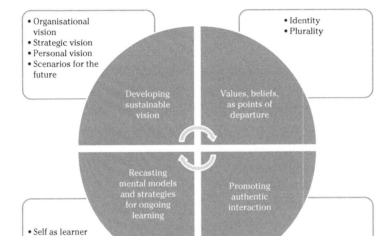

Results and benefits

This approach to leadership education has been practised at NUBS since 2011. It is a core module on the full-time MBA and around 50 students graduate each year engage with a social narrative of leadership that includes a strong emphasis on sustainability. It is available on the Executive MBA programme as an elective module and has been integrated into MSc elective modules that focus on strategy and leadership. It was delivered as an executive education module for the first time in 2012 and has, so far, been run with two cohorts of around 20 senior managers from large global companies. Feedback from students consistently affirms that the module challenges pre-existing ideas and helps them to appreciate the importance of soft skills in business and management and develop their capacity for reflective practice and self-awareness. One participant of an executive module remarked: '[The module was] really provocative and rewarding ... particularly interesting and holistic in its approach ... truly inspirational, informative and interesting. Thank you.'

Personal reflections submitted by the students also indicate that this approach to leadership prompts deep reflection on their ideas about leadership, management and sustainability.

The role of PRME/sustainability principles

The PRME initiative has added considerable weight to appeals for management education that supports a sustainable global society. The social narrative on leadership espoused by Starkey and Hall, developed through leadership scholarship and teaching practice at NUBS, argues for leadership education that attends to longer-term societal impacts, rather than short-term economic goals. Their perspective has strong resonance with the 'Purpose' Principle of PRME, which focuses on 'developing the capabilities of students to be future generators of sustainable value for business and society at large and to work for an inclusive and sustainable global economy'. It is also consistent with the Values and Methods Principles that focus on the ethos and processes of our educational frameworks. As such, the PRME provides a strong mandate for embedding sustainable leadership education into our programmes and supports engagement with our external partners on these issues.

References

Goleman, D. (2006) *Social Intelligence: The New Science of Human Relationships* (New York: Random House).

Hambrick, D. (1993) 'What If the Academy Actually Mattered?' *Academy of Management Review* 19: 11-16.

Kolb, D.A. (1984) *Experiential Learning* (Englewood Cliffs, NJ: Prentice Hall).

Mayer, J.D., and P. Salovey (1993) 'The Intelligence of Emotional Intelligence', *Intelligence* 17: 433-42.

Mintzberg, H. (2004) *Developing Managers Not MBAs* (London: FT Prentice Hall).

Snook, S.A., N.N. Nohria, and R. Khurana (eds.) (2012) *Handbook for Teaching Leadership: Knowing, Doing, and Being* (Thousand Oaks, CA: Sage).

Starkey, K., and C. Hall (2012) 'The Spirit of Leadership: New Directions in Leadership Education', in S.A Snook, N.N Nohria and R. Khurana (eds.), *Handbook for Teaching Leadership: Knowing, Doing, and Being* (Thousand Oaks, CA: Sage): 81-98.

Starkey, K., A. Hatchuel and S. Tempest (2004) 'Rethinking the Business School', *Journal of Management Studies* 41.8: 1521-31.

Zohar, D., and I. Marshall (2000) *Spiritual Intelligence: The Ultimate Intelligence* (London: Bloomsbury).

6 *San Patrignano, Italy:*
Land of cheese,
wine, and
self-discovery

Babson College

Babson Park, Massachusetts, United States

Introduction

An alumnus asked if Babson College could help the Community of San Patrignano (SP) become self-sufficient. San Patrignano, near Rimini, Italy, was created 35 years ago to help drug addicts recover. The organisation is 100% focused on providing a safe environment for the community at no cost to the participants or their families. The cost of food, shelter, medical care, and staff for 1,300 recovering drug addicts is €30 million, while the revenue from the sale of wine, cheese, furniture, textiles, meat, iron work, etc. offered by the community is €15 million. The community receives annual donations of €15 million, 80% of which is from one source.

The most profound aspect of San Patrignano is that participants are never left alone. They are always with their group and rise together, have breakfast, lunch, and dinner together, and go to work together. After dinner, the group decides between available options. An outside theatre shows news, followed by films and music. San Patrignano is not a prison. Participants can leave. However, other participants and staff go to great lengths to convince them to stay. For participants sent by the court, leaving would result in prison, so they tend to stay. Only 10% of the programme participants leave before completing the programme. Since its founding in 1978, San Patrignano has helped 20,000 individuals return to society. Over 70% do not return to drugs, compared to a success rate of 20–30% at other programmes.

This project did not easily fit into our current curriculum. It was not a traditional course or a traditional project sponsor. Babson treated this as a consulting project for the SP staff to give them processes to evaluate opportunities to grow revenue streams. Students were interviewed, and five students were selected. The mission given to the students was simple: develop a process for San Patrignano to become self-sustainable. The Babson MBA team would use their knowledge and skills to identify ways to reduce costs or increase revenues to eliminate the annual shortfall of €15 million. The project included four stages. First, the team spent one month researching non-profit business models. Second, the team and faculty adviser spent a week at San Patrignano interviewing staff and participants. Third, the team spent a month analysing the data collected and testing hypotheses; they then presented their final results to SP management.

Challenges

The students and faculty adviser travelled to the hills of Rimini for introductions. The participants enter the community in multiple ways. For some, it is an alternative to prison, while others are brought by their families and admit themselves. Programme participants are expected to detox before arriving. San Patrignano is a beautiful facility, in rolling hills with grapes, olives, horses, cows, pigs, and sheep. Entering the San Patrignano programme is a challenge. New arrivals must give up their money, gold and silver jewellery, cell phones, computers, and any other personal items. New arrivals are assigned to a participant who has been in the programme for 2–3 years. This person is mentor, coach, and keeper. The new arrival is also assigned to a work area and a group of participants. There are over 30 work areas including wine, cheese, bakery, graphic arts, horses, cows, pigs, carpentry, textiles, metalworking, meat preparation, wallpaper, and landscaping. San Patrignano assigns new arrivals to the work area that best suits the person and the needs of the community.

The current staff are very focused on the social aspect of returning former drug users to society. The staff have limited business experience or knowledge of cost and profit. The challenge of growing revenues faces a trade-off between volume of revenue and quality. For example, San Patrignano grows enough grapes to bottle 1,000,000 bottles of wine whereas this past year they only produced 400,000 bottles. The community could sell more wine, but some of the wine may be of a lesser quality. The headmaster of the wine work area feels that the increased volume may put too much pressure on the participants. A similar trade-off discussion was raised about cheese production.

The staff of San Patrignano are very dedicated to the mission of helping recovered drug users return to society. While management does not have skills such as budgeting, forecasting, marketing, distribution, etc., the MBA students were very impressed with their open and forthcoming responses to questions.

Actions taken

The MBA students returned to the United States to begin the process of examining costs and revenue, looking for opportunities. They examined the potential role of marketing to brand the products and use the social nature of San Patrignano to enhance the brand. The team also examined what management practices would better manage revenues and costs to move the community closer to self-sustainability. The team also examined how entrepreneurship training could be used in San Patrignano. Recommendations were presented to management as part of the overall sustainability of San Patrignano. Given a possible reduction of private funding, San Patrignano must become more self-sufficient. The recommended organisational changes were presented to increase revenues through better coordination of the commercial, purchasing, and business heads. Finally, the use of marketing skills was explained in the context of the US furniture market. San Patrignano is conducting a roadshow in eight US cities in May and June 2013, partially supported by the Babson recommendations.

Results and benefits

San Patrignano has launched a number of products based on the recommended market analysis. They have also evaluated all current products and services based on the model created to balance opportunities for programme participants when they leave with the market demand and profitability of each area.

Through cost reductions and increased revenue, the budget deficit should be reduced to €10 million in 2013.

The role of PRME/sustainability principles

- Use of management education to support programmes that reduce human suffering – helping San Patrignano become self-sufficient
- Cross-fertilisation of effective social programmes that can be used in multiple countries. San Patrignano's eight-city tour will highlight its successful programme for drug recovery in United States
- Students will learn how management education can be applied to non-profit organisations

Inspiring responsibility through the use of positive experiential exercises

University of Auckland

Auckland, New Zealand

Introduction

Contemporary education in the field of responsibility emphasises primarily intellectual issues and as such is largely *about* responsibility. A more effective process has to include a broader range of reinforcing intelligences, including moral intuition, observation, and emotion. The latter is particularly important for building a resilient commitment to responsible action and it is naive to believe that ethical action can be long maintained when it is felt to be futile or frustrating. In the real world, much irresponsibility stems from a feeling of powerlessness to effect positive change and/or believing that individual actions can have no impact. Such irresponsibility is maintained when we fail to realise the positive fulfilment that commonly accompanies more humane and considerate living. In this case story from the University of Auckland, two exercises are described that work to bring these thoughts and emotions to the surface, where they can be consciously addressed. These exercises are drawn from a collection designed to *inspire* positive change and further the core ideals of PRME by exemplifying creative curriculum design and delivery for a more globally responsible and sustainable world. The first works directly with the self-imposed barriers that learners confront when they try to act more responsibly, and the second with the positivity that comes from engaged and effective altruism.

Challenges

When talking with young business students about the future they want to see, they unanimously describe a world that is much more responsibly managed and, as a result, more sustainable, harmonious, inclusive, and thriving. Yet most also feel that, despite these aspirations, the reality of the near future will see declines on all of these dimensions. This is a depressing and deflating realisation, and education has a critical role to play in empowering young people to see that positive change not only *should* be, but *can* be made. Doing this requires that the personal barriers each learner uses to deny enacting a greater personal responsibility be brought to the surface, and that the benefits of taking action are experienced.

Actions taken

The first objective is aided hugely by an exercise in which students deny themselves the everyday indulgences that actively undermine the ideal world and reflect on the rationalisations that have resulted in abandoning responsible action. As students refrain from a whole range of 'irresponsible' purchases (generally successfully), potent dynamics are brought to the surface that reveal common patterns of debilitating resistance. When students work together to find shared themes that they commonly use in efforts to 'get off the hook', the majority mention being strongly tested by feelings of *futility* (I can't make a difference) and emotional *distance* (I can't relate to the problem).

As these deflating feelings of powerlessness emerge, partner exercises can be used. This allows students to actually make a difference to the lives of distant others by having partners act together to effect positive change. In its latest iteration, this involves working with a New Zealand charity, the Fred Hollows Foundation (FHF), which performs life-changing cataract operations in poor countries for $25 per eye. A spokesperson from the Foundation visits the class to debate issues and answer questions, and students are all given a 'cataract mask' that mimics what it is like to suffer from the ailment. Over the following week, they are challenged to ask four people they know for a $5 donation to the cause, adding $5 of their own if they so choose.

Results and benefits

Students write reflectively on the experience (as they do for the preceding exercise), recounting in detail their own thoughts and feelings and the reactions of those they approached for $5. After a week, students bring the accumulated money to class, where it is counted and handed over to the appreciative Foundation. The atmosphere in the classroom as students combine their money is incredibly inspiring, and the total is usually far greater than expected, as students use broader social networks to go beyond the strict requirements of the exercise. A class of 65 people will easily raise several thousand dollars, and the positive sense of responsible empowerment is deeply moving for all concerned. When combined, these two exercises allow the creative instructor to expose the core rationalisations that we use to excuse ourselves from engaging in more responsible action and allow a direct realisation of the emotional rewards of acting to change others' lives for the better.

To manage successfully for a better world, future leaders must be challenged to understand both the intellectual *and* the personal dynamics of responsible living. Over many years of using these and other exercises central to educating *for* responsibility, hundreds of students have described their experience as deeply 'transformative' and literally 'life-changing'.

The role of PRME/sustainability principles

This case story outlines a practical and inspiring classroom intervention that builds on a number of principles central to PRME's stated purpose, in particular:

- Principle 1, by developing the capabilities of students to work for an inclusive and sustainable global economy
- Principle 2, by centrally incorporating values of global responsibility
- Principle 3, by creating materials, processes and environments to enable effective and responsible learning experiences
- Principle 6, by facilitating and supporting dialogue with external organisations working for greater responsibility

8

Broadening views through teamwork

ESPOL-ESPAE Graduate School of Management

Guayaquil, Guayas, Ecuador

Introduction

ESPAE, created in 1983 as the first business school of Ecuador and based at Escuela Superior Politécnica del Litoral (ESPOL), emphasises leadership, innovation, entrepreneurship development, and application of information technology in business. At ESPOL-ESPAE Graduate School of Management, we believe that teamwork is critical when you value diversity and innovation. The experience that follows responds to the need to strengthen collaboration (1) among students, and (2) among faculty members and staff, under the assumption that working in teams facilitates the recognition of value in diversity, develops tolerance and acceptance, and most of all builds trust, which is indispensable for collaboration and inclusion.

Challenges

The ESPAE Mission states that the school should

> contribute to the improvement of managerial and business capacity of private, public, and non-profit organisations in Ecuador, as well as their integration into the global economy by providing graduate education to experienced

professionals that is focused on entrepreneurship, ethics, and social responsibility as core values. We enrich our education through applied research and the school participation in development projects and consulting.

Three axes of actions derive from the mission: entrepreneurship, global perspective, and social responsibility. We expect our curricular emphasis as well as our behaviour as a school to develop around those axes.

Actions taken

Study teams

After becoming signatory to PRME in 2007, ESPAE began organising study teams in 2008 composed of diverse and complementary members. For the conformation of study teams, we take into account demographics, the admission test, etc., and conduct team-building sessions at the beginning of each programme. We assist students with their conflict resolution during their master's. At the beginning the emphasis in study teams was in response to the need to develop soft skills in MBA and other specialised master's students, as well as encouraging teamwork as key skill for entrepreneurship and innovation.

Once the project of building study teams was in place and conflicts arose, we recognised a higher scope for the study teams – learning to find value in diversity. However, to exploit the benefits of study teams, we also needed to train our faculty. Our first thoughts were to encourage faculty to design the courses accordingly – develop team exercises, evaluate teamwork as well as individual work, and the like.

Faculty teams

During our faculty discussions, we discovered that they also needed to develop the ability to work in teams. We recognised that ethics and social responsibility are not silos. Consequently, it is important to promote discussion among faculty and encourage them to integrate such topics, through interdisciplinary collaboration, into diverse courses and research. In an effort to achieve this goal, a seminar on teamwork was conducted for faculty and staff members in September 2009. The objective of the workshop was to 'learn to apply tools that allow effective teamwork by students and encourage teamwork among faculty members'. The role of teams in education and research was also discussed.

Teamwork among professors brings value in extending or broadening the scope of their research, provides a better knowledge of societal problems, which generally require a multidisciplinary approach, and allows them to engage in development projects, etc.

Results and benefits

After four years we have improved the management of the study teams. In a recent focus group conducted with MBA alumni for a regional study, we found that they indeed value their team experience, their classmates, and the opportunities that they found through the networking that this form of organisation promoted. We have not evaluated the effectiveness of our faculty teamwork; however, we have seen more multidisciplinary work among faculty of economics and entrepreneurship, organisational behaviour, international business, and management education.

The role of PRME/sustainability principles

PRME helped to:

- Focus school decisions and actions
- Signal our values to our community
- Facilitate the achievement of our mission
- Facilitate dialogue with alumni

Section 2

Beyond the classroom
Scaling experiential learning

9

Wake up and smell the coffee: Developing students' understanding of Fairtrade through experiential learning

Leeds University Business School

Leeds, England, United Kingdom

Introduction

This case story describes how a module in Volunteering and Enterprise at Leeds University Business School was used to provide students with real-life experience of the work of Fairtrade (www.fairtrade.org.uk) through developing and managing their own entrepreneurial projects. Through their learning on the module, the students developed their potential to create sustainable value for business and society (Principle 1), delivering initiatives based on the values of global social responsibility (Principle 2). This case story presents an example of curriculum development based on Principle 3 of creating educational opportunities that enable effective learning experiences for responsible leadership.

The module was designed as part of the social enterprise stream of the University's modules in enterprise and students participating in the module came from a range of disciplines. The University's catering manager had championed Fairtrade within the University for several years, converting hospitality and catering provision to Fairtrade-sourced goods, but was keen to make the crossover from operational priorities into academic values by engaging students in Fairtrade initiatives. As such, the Business School was knocking at an open door when we approached her about building Fairtrade into a module.

Challenges

First, we were asking students who had until that point worked largely, or even exclusively, with for-profit models of business to shift to a values-based paradigm. This was addressed by acknowledging up front the module leader's own support for the Fairtrade mission and communicating to students that although they would have to engage in initiatives designed to promote Fairtrade values they were not expected to endorse them personally. In fact, as described below, many of the students did alter their values and attitudes as a result of taking the module.

Actions taken

The project brief tasked students with raising awareness about Fairtrade, and what it stands for, within the student population. Projects had to be self-sustaining and the remit we set was intentionally broad, because students had to assess ideas, find and talk to the relevant people, and work on their enterprise skills. Initiatives included getting involved with the Fairtrade Leeds Fashion Show, liaising with Fairtrade suppliers, selling Fairtrade goods on campus, and writing proposals suggesting how Fairtrade could be incorporated into modules in different subjects. They even formed a Fairtrade Society.

The University's Fairtrade Steering Group was so impressed with the projects that they sponsored an award enabling two students to visit Tanzania for a week. During the trip, the winners accompanied a Café Direct representative on a visit to a Fairtrade coffee plantation. They picked, ground, and drank their own coffee and met people who benefit from the Fairtrade system.

> Being given the opportunity to travel to Tanzania was amazing. Meeting the farmers behind the coffee beans was a strong reminder of the often forgotten individuals behind the Fairtrade initiative – seeing the human side of coffee production as opposed to the competitive commercial aspect of it which is what we had previously studied.

Results and benefits

Student feedback indicated that even those who were not lucky enough to go to Tanzania significantly changed their attitudes and values as a result of their learning to Fairtrade:

- A big change to me is that when I buy things, the first thing that I check is whether it is Fairtrade
- I encourage my friends to buy Fairtrade

Strikingly, this attitude and value change seems not to have been confined solely to Fairtrade, but the effects also spilled over to attitudes towards volunteering:

- Completing this module has altered my behaviour and my attitudes towards volunteering
- I will definitely continue volunteering. You get this sense of achievement which you can't really get from other activities

And to longer-term career ambitions:

- I realise that I don't want to be a part of one of these profit organisations that are really working for themselves. I would like to help and do something [with social value].

Looking forward, a rather more prosaic issue will be fitting the module's novel structure (originally based on day-long workshops with significant input from external stakeholders) into the University timetable. As such, we are having to compromise on structure when the module returns next year but hope that this will be worth it by making it accessible to a greater number of students.

The role of PRME/sustainability principles

- Principle 1: Providing students with opportunities to develop their potential to create sustainable value for business and society through experiential learning via real-life volunteering projects
- Principle 2: Incorporating values of global social responsibility directly into the learning materials and giving students opportunities to live these values through their work
- Principle 3: Designing the curriculum around real-life volunteering and an explicit values set

10 *Responsible management education using a study-trip pedagogy of risk and ethics*

University of the West of England Faculty of Business and Law

Bristol, England, United Kingdom

Introduction

The case story, from the Faculty of Business and Law at the University of the West of England, illustrates the pedagogic, ethical, and developmental aspects of introducing an annual study trip within the Faculty's MBA programme curriculum by reflecting on the experience of the students and staff during 2009–2012.

Challenges

The annual MBA study trip was introduced in 2009 to address, in a responsible way, a multinational multidisciplinary class, and the pertinent topics of sustainability, risk, crises, complexity, and security in a global context. It has aspired to provide a value-adding learning experience that combines traditional lectures and seminars with visits to specific locations and participation in consultancy projects for local partners (e.g. national parks and river protection; mining, tourism, and eco-tourism; small professional firms/consultancies). Disciplinary diversity of the academic team involved in the teaching of the module and organising the field trip provides a unique added value as it covers the fields of economics, politics, philosophy, law, management, sociology, and engineering. The trips were made possible through a partnership with the team managing the EU supported project 'Cross-European Danube Parks Protection Network' (see PRME biennial report, 2012).

Actions taken

The series of trips between 2009 and 2012 provided the students with an opportunity to engage with local organisations and academic institutions and gain 'hands-on' experience of privatisation, globalisation, economic transition, political life, and public policies in the region. It also facilitated first-hand appreciation of nature's intrinsic value and shared vulnerability by being in nature, as well as exposure, reflection, and a healthy respect towards sociocultural and ecological diversity and healthy relationships with others. The knowledge and hospitality of our hosts at each of the sites ensured an outstanding educational experience with the focus principally on global risk and sustainability issues.

By focusing from the very start on the values, the vulnerabilities, and the ideological struggle behind the sustainability crises and the proposed global and local solutions, it was our intention to create a rhetorical space for an emotional transitioning, a cognitive liberation, and a collective negotiation of shared reality among the students – one that disallowed the traditional ontological separation between economic and ecological spheres. Key challenges we faced were a combination of:

- 'Sustainability' and 'management' as non-homogenous subjects
- Micro-diversity in the class

- Vested/powerful interests, tradition, and expectations of what a 'responsible' MBA education might be
- Learning process laden with resistance and anxiety

A variety of pedagogic methods and tools were employed to allow for a much-needed space for collective and individual exposure to the ideas, and for reflection on real issues in the concrete local situations of the lived experience. The combination of specialist lectures and highly relevant visits, set against the background of a unique local culture, art, and history, made the educational experience especially effective and also highly enjoyable.

Results and benefits

The trip has been seen as an immensely valuable experience for all, summed up by one of the students as: 'A combination of amazing people, interesting lectures, flexible planning, intellectual input and open-mindedness that made this trip one that will never be forgotten.'

As part of a larger pedagogic project, a post-experience survey and individual interviews with participating students were conducted after each trip. All the quotes come from the resulting database. The illustrations and discussion below provide a fruitful foundation for addressing what in our view are the key questions.

Key discussion points

- How do we reorient the focus from sustainability to the complex moral problem of 'unsustainability' (the sustainability crisis), which inevitably invokes considerations of risk and ethics beyond and above the economic and scientific ones?
- How can we encourage pedagogy informed by moral philosophy to broaden the scope of the subject matter to

embrace concerns of values, vulnerabilities, ideological struggle, and (in)equality in context?

- How do we ensure that business education in this area encourages ethical addressing of both the causes and the solutions to the crisis without falling into a trap of dominant economic-technological drivers?

Projects

Visits to Donau-Auen National Park (Hainburg), an International Union for Conservation of Nature (IUCN) protected ecological sanctuary on the River Danube along the eastern border of Austria in 2009 and 2010 and to Djerdap National Park on the River Danube on the Serbian border with Romania in 2011, provided a unique learning environment. Eight collaborative consultancy projects, led by the students, were successfully completed as a result of our collaboration with the management teams of the national parks, of the Cross-European Danube Parks Protection Network and local communities and universities as per Principles 5 and 6 of the PRME. The collaborative consultancy projects were about:

- An analysis of internal and external communications within the EU-funded, complex collaborative DANUBE-PARKS project
- Sustainability and eco-tourism in parks along the river Danube – some guidelines for Donau-Auen and Djerdap National Parks
- Some recommendations for sustainable transport solutions in the context of Donau-Auen National Park
- Renewable energy, hydropower, ecology, and risks – a comparative study of global practices/feasibility study of the impact of opening a phosphate mine on environment and communities – risk, costs, and benefits – for Victoria Group, Serbia
- Sustainable business and knowledge economy for Yu-Build Consultancy, Belgrade, Serbia

- Collaboration challenges between Djerdap National Park and the Danube Parks Protection Network for the management of Danube Parks

The MBA students' comments on their experience show the impact of our pedagogic aim on their development towards building a shared understanding in a global context, focusing on values, humanity, and moral responsibility and considering alternatives in an informed manner:

> This was different, it was not just another module about global business, it was about the people who do the business globally and the problems and opportunities that they may face during their journey of working globally, and the success and failures of their decisions and its impact not only on the global economy but also on the global environment.

> The lectures and class discussions have opened up my awareness of decisions that I make both at work and at home and the impact of that decision. I feel that I have developed greater moral responsibility for the planet. I found myself getting very angry about global situations when writing my assignment.

> I have been interested in why, as a nation and even globally, we haven't woken up to the problems that are being talked about and are emerging as the years go by: being resourceful with waste; taking responsibility, being transparent about risks, thinking creatively about natural beauty, protection of the environment and business success away from pollutants and disregard. This trip broadened my awareness of these issues.

References

For more information on the Donau-Auen National Park (Hainburg), please visit: http://www.donauauen.at/?area=nationalpark
For more information on the Djerdap National Park, please visit: http://www.npd jerdap.org/en_index.html

11

On-campus social enterprises develop responsible leaders

Bentley University

Waltham, Massachusetts, United States

Introduction

The success of Bentley University's first social enterprise serves as a model for how business curricula (Principle 3) can create a continuing stream of opportunities for developing responsible leaders while, at the same time, building win–win partnerships (Principle 5) with 501(c)3 foundations (US tax-exempt non-profit organisations) engaged in social causes that the University community supports.

The Mmofra Trom Bead Project (MTBP) is staffed, managed, and operated by student volunteers who apply for roles just as one would apply for a paid position. The organisation has a CEO, COO, and CFO as well as several managerial positions that report directly to the three-person leadership team. The CEO is accountable to and a member of the Advisory Board to the Mmofra Trom Foundation (a US 501(c)3) and accountable to the University through a Bentley faculty supervisor, who is also on the Advisory Board that meets semi-annually. Vulnerable children at the Mmofra Trom Education Center in Ghana string recycled glass beads into bracelets that Bentley students sell, with profits paying for their high school and university fees. A $100 purchase of beads in 2008 led to a $50,000 Education Fund by 2013. Students get the satisfaction of 'giving the gift of education, one bracelet at a time'.

Challenges and actions taken

Sustainable opportunities

Two students who met the children of Mmofra Trom when they were freshmen became increasingly committed over four years' time. Understandably, they wanted to retain their leadership role after they graduated. MTBP had become 'their baby', even though the business was started by a Bentley faculty member. Bentley did not want to lose that commitment but did want the leadership opportunity to be available to other undergraduates. We met this challenge by appointing graduating CEOs as permanent members of the Advisory Board. Alumni leaders are responsible for long-range strategic planning, and each year a new CEO is appointed to the Board. This has had the added benefit of strengthening ties between the University and its alumni.

Academic credit adds incentive

To increase students' motivation for getting involved with the social enterprise, students can earn academic credit for their work for the social enterprise. The Advisory Board of the Mmofra Trom Foundation became a community partner with Bentley's Center for Service Learning and can submit specific projects to the Center. Depending on the academic skills that the project requires (international marketing, social media, sales management, etc.), the Center contacts faculty members who award students a 4th credit for a 3-credit course if they spend about two hours per week applying course-related skills to a specific community project.

Tax status and managing profits

Students who have started social enterprises of their own face the challenge of paying salaries and taxes. Other universities have described failures based on not being able to make enough profit once they covered all of their expenses, and not being able to figure out how to keep the money separate from university-owned bank accounts. Having the umbrella of a US Foundation is a vital component of the success of this model. Profits go into the Foundation's bank account, and the Foundation is responsible for wiring funds to Ghana to pay school fees and tuitions. MTBP has a meticulous accounting system, which the CFO maintains, and those records are presented to the Foundation's CFO for auditing. We do not have to charge taxes for bracelet sales since we have 501(c)3 status, and the Foundation takes care of IRS reporting each year. There is no complexity for the University's accounting and banking systems.

Results and benefits

Responsible leadership training

This opportunity gives students a chance to experience first-hand what it's like to hold a senior position in a business, and gives them a great deal of experience in managing and motivating their people while moving the business objectives forward. At the same time, they experience the satisfaction of using their business skills to accomplish a social objective – responsible leadership at its best. Similarly, service-learning students are using their business skills to make a genuine difference. Analysing case studies cannot compare to the learning value of working for a real business, where your recommendations are reviewed by a Board, and you can actually implement your ideas to see what kind of business results you get.

Encourages more social enterprises

Other students and faculty see the success of MTBP and are encouraged to start another social enterprise in support of community partners with 501(c)3 status. A local community association is working with Bentley students and faculty to create a business plan for unemployed teenagers to rake leaves and mow lawns to generate funds to support youth programmes. A team of students are writing a business plan to import medicinal herbs from a farmers' cooperative in a developing country. Bentley's positive experience with MTBP has opened the University's doors to social enterprises.

Low cost to the university

The cost to the University is 'low to none'. Faculty supervisors offer their time on behalf of the University to provide continuity and sustainability from year to year. Students get committed to causes, but they graduate. It takes the University's commitment to sponsorship to keep social enterprise opportunities on campus and available as part of the University's overall approach to developing responsible leaders. For several years the bracelet inventory was spread out in several dorm rooms. Eventually the University offered MTBP space for storing the inventory in one place, giving more visibility to Bentley's ongoing support of social enterprises at very little cost.

The role of PRME/sustainability principles

The Principles can provide the background inspiration for shaping the policies and practices surrounding University-sponsored social enterprises, such that the skill-building opportunities social enterprises represent formally support academic learning and are integrated into the curriculum. At the same time, the University ties to 501(c)3 entities that are working on social issues important to the campus community build valuable partnerships.

12

Into the wild: Pedagogical innovation for responsible management

Rotterdam School of Management Erasmus University

Rotterdam, The Netherlands

Introduction

A pedagogical innovation, an entire course at the European business school Rotterdam School of Management Erasmus University is taught outdoors, at a botanical garden. Companies in Ecologies is a master's elective offered at the Business–Society Management department. This case story relates how a professor has innovated at a business school by creating an outdoor course that is entirely given at a botanical garden outside the university.

Challenges

Increasingly, questions are raised about management education and how business school education could encourage responsible management. One criticism concerns the failure of business schools to help their students to connect to natural environment and ecological issues. From the literature we see that one of the wanted changes is that students would be more connected to the natural environment.

In 'An Interview with Education for Sustainable Development "Young Voices"', one of the voices explained that 'there is a lot to be done in terms of linking knowledge to actions' (Shealy 2009).

In the report *Educating for a Sustainable Future*, a national environmental education statement for Australian schools (Australian Government Department of the Environment and Heritage 2005) a clear distinction is made between education about the environment and *in* the environment: 'Education about the environment focuses on students' understanding of important facts, concepts and theories, while education *in* the environment involves students in direct contact with a beach, forest, street or park to develop awareness and concern for the environment.'

Muir (1996), who took a close look at business schools, explains that placing the students into 'real life' environments helps them 'to identify and challenge assumptions and values in the organisation, to highlight the context in which action and practices occur, and to explore alternatives to a given situation'.

Actions taken

The course was created in 2006 by Gail Whiteman, endowed professor of sustainability, management, and climate change.

When Whiteman was asked to create the course, she made a point of teaching it outdoors. For her, it had to be outdoors to help the students to connect to the natural environment that they were talking about. Whiteman describes the courses as experiential as well as linked to the business perspective. The students come to the garden twice a week over three months. They spend a few hours at the garden doing group projects, reflecting on various topics, and sharing ideas and concerns. They also visit the Interface Company, a carpet manufacturer aiming at zero carbon emission by 2030, and share management challenges towards sustainable and responsible purposes.

Besides the meetings, readings are posted online, which students are required to reflect on. They are also required to create a field journal that is

> reflective and personal in nature ... reflects upon the literature, the classes, the news, and their own life experiences to document their evolving understanding of sustainability, including their intellectual and emotional breakthroughs as well as their frustrations. Within the field journal, they should also start developing their 'ecosophy,' that is a set of questions or concerns (course outline 2007).

As Whiteman wants the students to use their 'multi senses' and not only their brain, she asks them to be creative, to take risks, and to be supportive. It is a highly participatory class where people are required to engage and participate in different ways, according to the various profiles. The final exam is not an exam, as Whiteman explains with a big smile on her face, but an artistic project. Each student has to try artistically and emotionally to relate to the topics.

Results and benefits

The first immediate result is to help students to reconnect to their natural environment. As Whiteman witnesses every year, students have pleasure coming here; some of them can be sceptical about the content or the use of the course at the beginning but they enjoy the place. During the first days of the MBA course given in 2012, we could hear students sharing with each other, 'It reminds me of my childhood. I used to love nature and play in it all the time.'

The artistic project, called 'photo essay', brings various results; some students grow awareness about their natural surroundings, they start to slow down, to walk more outside, to appreciate the weather and the fauna and flora around them, even in the city. Some students start to calculate their carbon footprint and build a strategy to lower it by different actions: using less water, walking or cycling more, lowering the heater.

In 2008, 13 MSc students took the course and wrote a field journal. In the field journals it is possible to read how the natural environment has a positive impact on the participants. Each student witnesses positive self-change. And many of them compare its positive impact to a traditional course taught inside a building. Witnessing the environmental impact, a student explained that,

> We all have had a moment of feeling completely connected, entangled and intertwined with nature. It's this moment of feeling part of this web of life that could provide us the energy to change our ways of living. In other words, 'there's an "I" in responsibility' and we should become more aware of that.

Regarding the impact of the class compared to a traditional one, another student mentioned after class 12,

> This course has been very different from any other course I have taken before, but the impact has been so much bigger. I can't recall one course that really made me think about myself and the course material as much as this course has. I believe this course did not only benefit my academic development, but it has also been a great personal experience, thank you.

The role of PRME/sustainability principles

- **Principle 1:** Throughout the course, students change their perception about business and the impact of businesses on the natural environment
- **Principle 2:** The companies and ecology course incorporates the values of global social responsibility as portrayed in international initiatives, such as the United Nations Global Compact

- **Principle 5:** The course is open to various guest speakers and the students visit companies and have the opportunity of interacting with managers of business corporations to explore effective approaches to meeting challenges about sustainable and responsible management

References

Australian Government Department of the Environment and Heritage (2005) *Educating for a Sustainable Future* (Canberra: Department of the Environment and Heritage).

Shealy, C. (2009) 'An Interview With Education for Sustainable Development "Young Voices": Beliefs and Values From the Next Generation of ESD Leaders', *Beliefs and Values* 1.2: 131-34.

13

Who said corporate governance can't be fun? Extracurricular activities as learning tools

The American University in Cairo School of Business

Cairo, Egypt

Introduction

The Corporate Governance Club (CGC) at the American University in Cairo (AUC) School of Business is the first Egyptian student-based academic club that is dedicated to the dissemination of corporate governance principles and best practices among students. It aims at encouraging interdisciplinary dialogue among students of business, finance, economics, law, and accounting who share a common interest in working in a fair and transparent corporate environment. The CGC was established in 2010 with the mission of 'Promoting corporate governance literacy, enhancing the notion of business ethics, increasing the awareness of the tools of combating corporate financial corruption and emphasizing the importance of financial transparency.'

Challenges

The importance of corporate governance in today's business world dictates that graduates of business schools understand and appreciate means of responsible management of business through legal compliance, ethical business practices, shareholder value maximisation, and maintaining market trust. Due to the multifaceted nature of governance, its topics are covered piecemeal in different courses, such as business ethics, law, management, auditing, and finance, to name a few. In many instances, the 'legalities' of governance are more pronounced than its other dimensions, making it less interesting for many business students. The CGC was established in an attempt to provide a comprehensive coverage of governance topics that balances across its legal, business, ethical, and social dimensions in ways that are not confined to the typical in-class pedagogical tools.

Actions taken and results

The CGC devised a variety of interesting and appealing activities that targeted students from AUC and other Egyptian universities, both public and private. In addition, as part of its outreach efforts, the CGC launched the CGC Ambassador Program during 2011–12. This programme aims at expanding the scope of CGC by establishing a network of representatives in governmental and private academic institutions. CGC ambassadors act as liaisons between the CGC-AUC team and CGC members in other universities. The following is a brief description of the main activities of the club during 2010–13.

CGC corporate governance competitions

The CGC held three competitions in October 2010, October 2011, and March 2012. These competitions consisted of three segments. First, an opening session that featured keynote speakers, such as the Chairman of the Egyptian Stock Exchange, the Executive Director of the Egyptian Institute of Directors, the Executive Director of the Center for Transparency, the Chairman of the Egyptian Financial Supervisory Authority, faculty members, and partners in leading auditing firms. Second, training sessions covered such topics as the agency problem, the functions of the board of directors, the importance of disclosure and transparency, the protection of shareholders' rights, and the legal and technical frameworks of corporate fraud. Third, a qualifying exam, followed by a speed-based competition in front of a live audience. Top winners were awarded monetary prizes, and all participants received certificates of attendance. The average number of participants in these competitions was 100 students from AUC and other public and private Egyptian universities.

CGC workshop 'Combating Money Laundering: An Introduction'

Two 6-hour CGC workshops were delivered to more than 100 undergraduate and graduate students from AUC, Ain Shams University, and Cairo University in April 2011 with a re-run in May 2011. The workshop addressed the area of money laundering, a topic that is relevant to today's global market but is unlikely to be covered in any undergraduate course. The workshop focused on how proceeds of crime are laundered and what could be done to mitigate such practices. Participants were able to interact with leading experts from the Money Laundering Combating Unit, the financial intelligence unit of the Central Bank of Egypt.

CGC lecture 'Combating Corporate Corruption'

This one-hour lecture was part of the School of Business Seminar Series 'Transforming Egypt' in April 2011. The lecture focused on responsible management, cases of corporate fraud, and means of deterrence. The lecture was presented by the Executive Director of the Center for Transparency.

CGC 'board games'

Through partnership with PricewaterhouseCoopers (PwC), this signature activity is a simulation of board of directors (BOD) meetings that involves students role-playing the various constituents of the board, namely the chief executive officer, the board chairperson, a major shareholder director, an independent director, and a board secretary. The simulation involved seven teams of five members. The 35 participants attended an introductory workshop on the BOD, how it functions, and the role of each member. The workshop was delivered by a corporate governance expert from PwC. At the end of the workshop the participants received an 'informational file' that featured background information about a hypothetical company and description of the different scenarios that could face the boards. The teams were given a week to practise these scenarios. In the first round, all teams simulated a BOD meeting addressing a 'basic' scenario. The meetings were recorded and judges reviewed them to select the best three boards in terms of board dynamics and the quality of the decision-making process. Each one of the top three boards randomly selected a different 'advanced' scenario, which was simulated in front of the judges and a live audience. At the conclusion of the event, awards were granted to the top three boards and to selected individual members who demonstrated exceptional performance.

The role of PRME/sustainability principles

- The CGC provides innovative means for disseminating concepts and applications of a responsible management notion (i.e. corporate governance)
- The CGC collaborates with governmental, civic, and business entities, which provide technical and/or financial support for its activities
- The CGC engages experts in the area of corporate governance and other related fields to share experiences with students and to shed light on timely issues related to responsible business practices at large

14

First Steps in CSR programme: Good managers, better Colombians

Externado University of Colombia

Bogotá, Colombia

Introduction

The promotion of social responsibility in the business environment is not an easy enterprise. It takes more than just knowledge application, methods, tools, or budget. It takes persistence and institutional will, since the creation of behavioural modification and transformation of mind-set requires efforts and commitment for the long term.

With over 5,400 undergraduate students, 2,800 post-graduates, significant publication and research, and over 45 years of tradition, the Faculty of Business Administration of the Externado University of Colombia is committed to the integral development of managers who are capable of taking on the challenges of the 21st century. With the initiative First Steps in CSR programme, Externado, with the partnership of the Global Compact Network Colombia, address this important challenge through students, professors, small and medium enterprises (SMEs), big company signatories of the Global Compact, and other institutions, such as unions and business associations.

Challenges

Even though the issue of corporate social responsibility is not new in Colombia and is currently recognised as a major commitment from the various institutions that promote it, many companies are still not familiar with the concept of social responsibility or its implication for a company's operation, especially in SMEs.

Studies such as the Inter-American Development Bank and IKEI (2005), the Colombian Centre for Social Responsibility and IPSOS (2006), and the survey of the National Business Association of Colombia (ANDI), which has been doing this survey since 2004, show, respectively, how between SMEs there exists a medium and low level of implementation of CSR activities in Latin America, less knowledge and implementation of CSR in comparison with large companies, and obstacles such as lack of knowledge of the topic or associated costs, and lack of allies and cooperation.

Data demonstrates the importance of opening spaces for awareness, promotion, training, and support for entrepreneurs in the country, particularly SMEs. This is especially important because the SME sector, according to studies such as ESSER (1996) and SNIJDERS (2003), is essential to the development of a country, in part due to its high capacity for job creation, increased efforts in generating GDP, and export growth.

Actions taken

To address this issue, 2006 saw the convergence of different efforts in the circuit of teaching, research, and extension, resulting in the First Steps in CSR programme. This programme is a cooperation exercise and generation of synergies between academia, business, and institutions, in which students trained as junior consultants, and accompanied by expert instructors in CSR, provide specialised technical advice that impacts the management of SMEs.

For this, we constructed a series of methodologies, protocols, and tools that facilitate the realisation of a complex exercise – consulting outside the university, but with the same academic rigour and building trust among all stakeholders.

Despite high acceptance by students and teachers, implementing this initiative brought certain difficulties, including the need for other resources, coordination of different actors and, in particular, the lack of interest in participating by SMEs.

These difficulties were gradually resolved by generating new instruments and cooperation agreements with different public and private organisations. However, the active and fluid participation of SMEs was achieved through the agreement with the Global Compact Network Colombia in 2011 and the strategy of linking companies in the supply chain of a large corporation.

During the programme, participant entrepreneurs identify the status of their company compared to major international conventions of social responsibility, define their stakeholders and their main expectations, and initiate an improvement process that seeks to strategically meet the business goals and enable them to improve their performance in social responsibility in the short and medium term.

Results and benefits

Up to December 2012, the programme has yielded the following results:

- Linking of large companies, such as Petrobras, ENDESA, ETB, and Pacific Rubiales
- Participation of 220 SMEs and 525 students (386 undergraduate and 139 post-graduates)
- Cooperation with institutions such as Confecamaras, Chambers of Commerce of Bogotá, Medellín, Cali, Barranquilla and Cartagena, the IADB, and the IMF, ASOCOLFLORES,

Colsubsidio Fenalco Bogotá, SENA, and the Superintendence of Companies
- Construction of intervention methodologies CSR in SMEs
- Providing virtual platform support to consultants
- Publication of documents, articles, and CSR methodologies, in partnership with several other institutions, such as the Guide to Responsible Business for SMEs, published in conjunction with Confecamaras, the IMF, the IADB, Proexport, and the Ministry of Social Protection, among others

For the students:

- Improves the quality and relevance of the training provided by the university
- Raises awareness for their work as future managers
- Gives them advantages in the job market, based on knowledge and practical experience

For the entrepreneurs:

- Raises awareness of the social impact of their management and their responsibilities as managers
- Lets them know of risks and opportunities for their business
- Offers concrete improvements in the short and medium term

For the faculty:

- Promotes the value of these methods
- Links them with today's business reality
- Strengthens research and social projection

For the Global Compact Network Colombia:

- Strengthens its academic offerings and incidence of positive action
- Promotes the institutional mission of corporate responsibility
- Links new businesses to the Global Compact

For more information, visit: http://190.7.110.123/irj/portal/anony mous/fac_administracion_empresas/fae/facultad/rse/primerospasos

The role of PRME/sustainability principles

The First Steps in CSR programme is expected to:

- Continue raising awareness, changing learning and behaviour among students and participating employers, and expanding coverage nationally, in partnership with the Global Compact Network Colombia and institutions operating regionally
- Publish practical tools, including a book, on responsible supply chains, with reference to practices in the region, in agreement with the Regional Centre for Latin America and the Caribbean, and in support of the Global Compact
- Continue efforts to generate institutional synergies that raise awareness, discuss and seek opportunities for joint work, including the Diploma Course in Business and Human Rights (openly offered to entrepreneurs by the University Externado of Colombia and the Global Compact Local Network), roundtables of the Global Compact Network Colombia, and other initiatives, such as the mirror committee of ISO 2600, the Colombian CSR Guide with the ICONTEC, Inclusive Business Bureau with CECODES, and participation on the editorial board of the journal *RS* (responsibility/sustainability)
- Continue with efforts to promote public debate on the challenges of social responsibility in different institutions and scenarios, such as forums and meetings including, for 2013, the planned participation as event organisers of the II Colombia Global Compact Congress, the academic and fair event 'Colombia Responsible,' and the Second Congress of Ethics and Social Responsibility, involving entities from all sectors

References

Colombian Center for Corporate Responsibility, CCRE, Ipsos – Napoleon Franco. 2006. Baseline Corporate Social Responsibility in Colombia. Bogotá. Available at: http://www.deres.org.uy/home/descargas/investigaciones/ESTUDIO_de_linea_de_base_de_RSE_2006_Centro_Colombiano_de_Responsabilidad_Empresarial.pdf. Accessed July 2013.

ESSER, Klaus. HILLERBRAND, Wolfgang. MESSNER, Dirk. MEYER-STAMER, Jorg. 1996. *Systemic Competitiveness: New Governance Patterns for Industrial Development*, GDI Books, Series No 7. London.

Vives, Corral, Isasi. 2005. *Corporate Social Responsibility in SMEs in Latin America*. Inter-American Development Bank. IKEY. Bogotá. Available at: http://www.mific.gob.ni/LinkClick.aspx?fileticket=L1R3XGBj7fA%3D&tabid=499&language=es-NI. Accessed July 2013.

National Association of Industrialists of Colombia – ANDI. 2012. *Corporate Social Responsibility Survey 2012*. Bogotá. Available at: http://www.andi.com.co/pages/proyectos_paginas/proyectos_detail.aspx?pro_id=69&Id=6&clase=8&Tipo=3. Accessed July 2013.

SNIJDERS, Jacqueline. 2003. *The SMEs in Focus: Main Results of the Observatory of European SMEs 2002*, Oficina de Publicaciones Oficiales de las CC.EE. Luxemburgo.

15

Engaging students in action learning about sustainability management

Lagos Business School Pan-Atlantic University

Lagos, Nigeria

Introduction

A module on Sustainability Management was introduced into the Senior Management Programme at Lagos Business School. The category of the students – senior managers in top organisations – required a teaching approach that would really make them engage with the topic and be moved to act. In order to achieve this, traditional and new media (PowerPoint presentations, radio jingles, TV ads, and Twitter) were incorporated into the usual case teaching method, and the students were challenged to be the protagonists of the message of sustainability. The module consisted of four sessions of 75 minutes each.

Challenges

Here and now, in the 21st century, it is time to bring multimedia and social media into the classroom. The first challenge was to get the classroom Internet-ready, but there was an administrative communication breakdown, and resolution took some time.

Beyond the use of technology, there was an interesting debate about which aspects of sustainability were more important and should therefore be given priority for class discussion. A main concern was that people issues in Nigeria override environmental issues and need to be addressed first. Other issues included the integration of personal responsibility and corporate responsibility as well as the role of government.

Actions taken

The students were asked to work in groups. Each group had to do research on sustainability and present it in PowerPoint followed by a panel discussion to the class. The topics for the groups were:

- Making a case for sustainable management in Nigeria and wider Africa
- Deep insights into the economic rewards of managing sustainably
- Fighting for social sustainability: where do people stand in the profit-people-planet spectrum?
- Management and the Earth: there is no Planet B

In addition, each group was expected to prepare:

- A radio jingle educating the public on sustainability (2 minutes maximum duration)
- A TV advert for a product/service (selected from one of their companies in the group) that emphasises its *green* aspects (5 minutes maximum duration). The aspects could be actual or potential

Finally, a 'twitclass' (via Twitter) was held to discuss one of the cases given to the students: Green Forests Inc.

Results and benefits

Each group did brilliant work. They engaged within their groups and made deep and insightful presentations to the whole class. The sessions were very participatory, and others who were not in the presenting group benefited and contributed to enriching discussions. The radio jingles and TV ads also came out very well and could be used to spread the message of sustainability. The class decided to pursue this possibility and also to initiate a tree-planting project. The 'twitclass' was successful – two of the students later offered free consulting services to the case subject. A number of the students continued the discussion on Twitter even after the class. Other expected results include:

- The airing of at least one of the radio jingles or TV ads
- Continuous advocacy for management for sustainability by the participant students
- Further assistance (advisory services and network reach) provided to the case subjects

Learning points

- The sessions were enjoyable and, at the same time, full of content. The students were happy to create and share knowledge themselves and put in the needed effort to do a good job. In the process, they assimilated principles of sustainability to a greater extent than might have been if they had passively attended lectures.
- The rich experience of the individual participants (senior managers from different industries) came out easily and was shared with everyone else
- The students learnt to articulate their stance on issues regarding sustainability and to reach out to others and talk about sustainability

The role of PRME/sustainability principles

This project draws on five of the Six Principles of PRME:

- The students' capacities regarding responsible management have been enhanced. Through testing and employing their creativity, the students' happiness at the end was palpable.
- Introducing the sustainability module supported sustainability values teaching at Lagos Business School
- The interactive teaching method was engaging and effective
- Since the participants are senior managers in Nigeria's top organisations, their discussions gave insights into the shared challenges that organisations face in the quest to achieve sustainable management
- Discussions on Twitter were a good beginning to dialogue between educators and students

Section 3

Beyond the business school

Mainstreaming PRME across HEIs

16

PRME beyond the business school

Aston University

Birmingham, England, United Kingdom

Introduction

The focus to date for implementation of PRME has primarily (and rightly) been on business and management schools; yet, if we think about the range of professions, businesses, and organisations that graduates go on to work in (and many of them in management positions), it is important to consider how the Principles of PRME can be used to influence the strategy of all programmes, particularly in relation to ethics, responsibility, and sustainability.

In 2007–08, a review of the Aston Business School curriculum was undertaken in order to provide a base line of information to enable progress to be made towards all business graduates becoming 'literate in social responsibility and sustainability'. This review aimed to determine the content and delivery of ethics, social responsibility, and sustainability provided for Business School students. To this end, module outlines for the postgraduate (MSc and MBA) and undergraduate programmes were scrutinised for explicit reference to the subjects, and curriculum maps were developed. Following the review, recommendations were made for changes, including new modules, inclusion of these issues in the placement year report, and the development of a new MSc in

Social Responsibility and Sustainability. These recommendations have all now been implemented.

In 2012, Aston University was developing its strategy towards 2020 and discussions centred on the integration of ethics, social responsibility, and sustainability as part of the new strategy in all aspects of University life.

Challenges

Social responsibility and sustainability (and related issues) are of concern for private, public, and third-sector organisations, professional bodies, community groups, and individual citizens locally, nationally, and internationally, and its importance for the global economy is likely to increase as the global indicators relating to resource exploitation, global poverty and inequality, climate change, species extinction, energy consumption (especially fossil fuels), etc., continue to be serious cause for concern. Therefore, it is important that all students at the University are equipped with the relevant knowledge and understanding of current and future implications for businesses and these other groups. As managers/ leaders of the future, all graduates will be required to be social responsibility and sustainability literate in order to directly address and make decisions regarding societal challenges in these areas.

Actions taken

The University 2020 Strategy was developed with social responsibility and sustainability as one of the eight key strategic aims.

The strategy states:

- **Aim 07:** Sustainability and social responsibility are issues our staff, students and stakeholders feel passionately about, and are central to how we work at the University, and how we relate to the world around us. Sustainability and social responsibility are based on ethical values and underpinned by the idea of economic, social, and environmental obligations to our range of stakeholders

- **07.01:** Commitment to the United Nations backed Principles of Responsible Management Education (PRME). Improving the integration of sustainability and social responsibility by embedding our activities in this area into all aspects of University life
- **07.03:** Social responsibility and sustainability literacy. Extending across the University curriculum changes aimed at enabling all graduates to be 'literate in social responsibility and sustainability'

The Curriculum Research Project aimed to provide an overview of the extent to which ethics, social responsibility and sustainability (and related topics) were already included in the curriculum across the University to enable individual schools to develop plans for any future changes they wish to make. The project researcher worked on mapping the curriculum for individual schools, using the methodology adopted by the Business School in its original review in 2008 (an update of the Business School review of the curriculum was also completed as part of the University project).

Results and benefits

The outcome of the project provided a base line of information about the curriculum in each school to enable progress to be made towards all graduates becoming 'literate in social responsibility and sustainability'. The first stage of the project, which involved a review at the module level, has been completed for all schools, and interim reports have been produced. The second stage of the project involves developing curriculum maps for each of the programmes within individual schools. This will enable the schools to have an overview of their respective students' access to content in this area in order to make plans for development of the curriculum in relation to ethics, social responsibility, and sustainability.

The role of PRME/sustainability principles

- The Business School became signatory to PRME in 2008 and has been actively engaged in a variety of PRME events and activities, which contributed to influencing the development of the University strategy
- The fact that there had been a successful curriculum project on the integration of ethics, social responsibility, and sustainability in the Business School provided a 'blueprint' for extending this across all schools in the University. It also provided a persuasive case for research funding to use the same methodology utilised in the Business School review
- Although not a PRME 'Principle' the statement following the principles: 'We understand that our own organisational practices should serve as examples of the values and attitudes we convey to our students', became an important part of the University strategy of 'integrating these issues into all aspects of University life'. This included the development of a University-wide Ethical Framework that integrates values and underpins changes in the curriculum (see Case 17 in this volume)

17

*Developing a
university-
wide ethical
framework*

Aston University
Birmingham, England, United Kingdom

Introduction

This case story outlines the development of Aston University's
Ethical Framework, which is an important part of the University
strategy of 'integrating [sustainability] issues into all aspects of
University life'. This case is therefore related to Principle 1 Purpose
and Principle 2 Values. Although not a PRME 'principle' the statement that follows the Principles – 'We understand that our own
organisational practices should serve as examples of the values
and attitudes we convey to our students' – is critical to developing
the values and culture of the institutions educating the future leaders of business and other organisations globally.

Challenges

The global environment within which the University operates is
characterised by increasing change, ambiguity, and uncertainty,
and the ways in which members of the University operate have
become more complex and regularly present new regulatory, ethical, and legal challenges. This was highlighted by the publication

of *The Woolf Inquiry: An Inquiry into the London School of Economics' Links with Libya and Lessons to be Learned* in October 2011.

In developing its strategy towards 2020, the University set out its plans to integrate ethics, social responsibility, and sustainability into all aspects of University life. In light of this, the University Executive and Governing Council considered the Woolf report and agreed on an action plan to clarify its ethical vision and state clearly its principles, values, and responsibilities. As part of this initiative, a working group was established to oversee the production of an Ethics Framework and review related policies and practices.

The Framework aim was to underpin the University's commitment to high ethical standards and regulatory compliance, and to set out the broad range of regulations, policies, and practices that govern its relationships with colleagues, customers, partners, suppliers, and other stakeholders. It would set out the ethical standards expected of all members of the University in everything they do and wherever they operate. The Framework would be supported by the more detailed policies referenced from the document and, where appropriate, policies determined locally and tailored to the individual requirements of each school or department. The Framework would provide information to help all members of the University community to make good, informed business decisions and to act on them with integrity. It would also provide advice on who to approach for advice when they are facing ethical dilemmas.

Actions taken

The Ethics Framework has been developed and is supported by web-based information on Areas of Activity and Ethics Resources. The contents of the Framework are as follows:

1. Introduction from the Vice-Chancellor
2. Guiding principles and values. (These reflect those of the Nolan Committee Principles of Standards in Public Life.

The principles include selflessness, integrity, objectivity, accountability, openness, honesty, and leadership)
3. Purpose and use of the Ethics Framework
4. Our values
5. How to determine if something is unethical
6. Where to go for help and advice on ethical issues
7. 'X' University as an ethical organisation
8. Responsibility for the Ethics Framework
9. Gifts and donations

A leaflet on the Ethics Framework has been developed focusing on the key messages. A video has also been produced to raise awareness about the Ethics Framework among all members of the University community and will be used in staff and student induction and as part of staff development activities.

A Good Governance Group has been systematically reviewing relevant University policies and procedures in the light of the ethical principles and values expressed in the above Ethics Framework and current best practice.

The working group involved in developing the Ethics Framework will also be reporting on further actions to improve awareness of ethical values and principles such as: induction of new staff and the training, guidance, and updating of existing staff, and how ethics, social responsibility, and sustainability are covered in the curriculum for all students.

Results and benefits

The Ethics Framework aims to embed the University's ethical values and principles into all activities and to guide behaviour of members of the University. It is intended to complement existing ethics-related policies, procedures, and codes of conduct and practice, which are now listed on the University Ethics Resources website. The framework outlines the key areas in which ethical considerations may arise and sets out the responsibilities of individuals, groups, committees, and other bodies in these areas.

All spheres of University life and activities have the potential to raise ethical concerns, from learning, teaching, and research to enterprise/commercial activity, financial transactions, student recruitment, staff–student relationships, membership of and behaviour in an academic community, alumni relations, donations, and award of honours.

The Ethics Framework is intended to guide members of the University in how to act properly with impartiality, integrity, good conscience, and judgement at all times. It provides support and guidance to staff, students, members of the governing body, and other stakeholders in their consideration of ethical issues arising from University activities and information about where individuals facing ethical dilemmas can seek further assistance and more detailed guidance in relation to particular spheres of activity. It is designed to become part of the way the University operates.

The role of PRME/sustainability principles

- Becoming a signatory to PRME has led to a systematic review of strategies, policies, and practices. The development of the Ethical Framework is part of this review process.
- PRME provides the context and 'legitimises' embarking on initiatives that may otherwise not be addressed.

18 *Issues around embedding PRME across a large multidiscipline faculty*

Coventry University Faculty of Business, Environment and Society

Coventry, England, United Kingdom

Introduction

The Business School at Coventry University has had a long-standing commitment to PRME, being one of the original signatories in 2007. However, the Business School sits within a much larger Faculty of Business, Environment and Society (BES) that includes the Law School and a range of social science, environmental science and humanities discipline areas. The Faculty has about 8,000 students with the Business School comprising just over half the student body. This unique combination of discipline areas is reflected in the Faculty's four main research centres, which operate on a multidisciplinary cross-Faculty basis. The four centres undertake research and consultancy in areas related to food security (CAFS), peace and reconciliation (CPRS), economic development and regeneration (SURGE), and social justice (CSR). The issues discussed in this case story relate to how to connect the sustainability-related work of the research centres to the teaching on the main courses and how to spread consideration of PRME out of the Business School to courses across the whole Faculty.

Challenges

First, how to address the current disconnect between the Faculty's research centres and teaching programmes. Although all the Faculty's departments have research groups/clusters that impact on their courses there is only minimal contact between the departments and the cross-Faculty research centres. Given the nature of the research undertaken in these centres there is currently a significant missed opportunity to enrich the content of courses with current 'live' research and sustainability-related case studies.

Second, the decision to spread PRME beyond the Business School recognises the fact that many graduates from the non-business courses actually progress to management-related careers similar to those from the Business School courses. In addition, there is a growing expectation from all students that issues related to sustainability are addressed in their courses. However, the specific challenge to be addressed is the need to develop a Faculty-wide view of sustainability that all the discipline areas feel they can relate to their courses.

Actions taken

To address the disconnection between the Faculty research centres and the courses a small group has been formed consisting of representatives from the research centres and teaching staff from the departments. The direct involvement of research centre staff in courses through lectures and presentations was dismissed on the grounds of organisational practicalities and probable lack of student engagement. A more realistic and effective means is seen to be through the development of multimedia resource packs by the research centres. These will be stand-alone resources that course teams can use in a number of ways to fit the needs of their course.

In many ways the second challenge is more difficult. The commonly used standard definitions of sustainability tend to reflect a specific discipline focus. The same applies to the Principle 1, which reflects the business and management basis from which PRME has been developed. Staff and students on the Business School's courses readily see the relevance of P1 to their courses; however, the same could not be said for staff and students involved with most courses in the non-Business School part of the Faculty. The decision was made not to take the obvious route and try to develop a definition of sustainability with which all areas of the Faculty feel comfortable. Instead the solution to be adopted has a more student-focused approach. This will take the form of the Faculty adopting as a principle that all students can expect that their courses will provide opportunities for them to engage with issues around sustainability. The nature of the engagement will vary according to discipline area. The precise wording of what will be a student 'statement of entitlement' will be developed in conjunction with all areas of the Faculty, both staff and students, to ensure maximum buy-in and commitment.

As a follow-on to the adoption of a student 'statement of entitlement', and to effectively embed PRME across the Faculty, all course teams will be required to produce a course-specific Self Improvement Plan (SIP). The course-level SIP will become part of our existing course review process. By this means consideration of PRME will also become part of the Faculty's formal reporting structure through Boards of Study and Faculty Board.

Results and benefits

The benefits for the Faculty will be a bringing together of our cross-Faculty research centre with departments with a resulting increased awareness of each other's work. However, more importantly, teaching staff and students will have the opportunity to explore issues around sustainability that are research/practice informed and contextualised within their discipline area.

One early result of discussing the PRME approach with non-Business School course teams has been the recognition of how students can engage with issues of sustainability within the context of their courses. Thus, for example, the Faculty's history degrees now have a mandatory final year module in Environmental History while English students examine the development of 'sustainability' as a discourse and through the use of metaphor.

The role of PRME/sustainability principles

For the Faculty PRME is important:

- As a means of connecting the wide range of sustainability-related research undertaken within the Faculty, to the Faculty's courses
- As a means to facilitate a discussion within the non-business part of the Faculty on how sustainability relates to their discipline area
- By expanding discussion of PRME beyond the Business School it re-emphasises 'sustainability' as one of the key underlying concepts on which the Faculty is based

19

Orienting the institution towards social debate

ESADE Business School Ramon Llull University

Barcelona, Spain

Introduction

Social debate is one of ESADE's missions. The institution aims to exercise its social influence in a responsible manner in order to contribute to public debate, act as a platform for the transfer of knowledge, and also to encourage and facilitate reflection and dialogue with and between stakeholders.

ESADE is a meeting point for numerous entrepreneurs, managers, academics, legal experts, politicians, and representatives of civil society. Around 80,000 people take part in the more than 1,100 events organised by the institution each year, many of which are in collaboration with ESADE alumni.

Two significant examples of social debate in 2012 at ESADE are:

- The Presentation of the Third Report of the Observatory on Spanish Multinational Companies (OEME): *Challenges for the Future of Spanish Multinationals*, written by ESADE in collaboration with ICEX, PwC Foundation, and the Banesto Foundation
- The VII Conference, offering reflection and discussion in Sant Benet de Bages, entitled 'Transformed by the Crisis.

From Resistance to Transformation: A Change that Can Be Positive' by the ESADE Chair in Leaderships and Democratic Governance, in collaboration with Caixa Catalunya

Challenges

When she began her mandate in September 2010, the Director General of ESADE, Eugenia Bieto, expressed her wish to continue to progress in order to create an increasingly socially responsible academic institution.

In order to integrate ESADE's social responsibility (SR) into the Institutional Strategic Plan, the Director General convened a task force made up of experienced ESADE managers and professors to reflect on this issue and draw up a Social Responsibility Master Plan (SR-ESADE) for 2011–14.

The basic aim of ESADE's SR Master Plan is to help achieve the objectives set by ESADE for 2020: 'To be a globally recognised academic institution, which inspires and prepares individuals and organisations to develop innovative, socially responsible leadership in order to build a better future.'

In order to achieve this, ESADE used one of its own models (Losada, Martell, and Lozano 2011), which, in a systemic and cross-cutting manner includes all the strategic areas – training, research, and social debate – as well as organisational culture and institutional policies.

ESADE is present in social debate through the talks, conferences, seminars, and forums it organises, the prizes it awards, the reports, studies, and proposals it prepares and broadcasts, its alliances and associations with other stakeholders, as well as through the opinion articles it publishes and the impact it makes in the national and international media, etc. The institution has also become one of the leading Spanish business schools in terms of the number of opinion pieces published in the international press.

After a comprehensive analysis and diagnosis of the social debate (typology of events, topics, media impact, etc.) was carried out, it was concluded that there was a need to create the social debate strategy at ESADE.

The principal challenges of this are:

- To rethink the social debate model
- To strengthen the synergies of all social debate actions with research and training activities
- To assess the impact of the various actions

Actions taken

Step 1: Preparation

The General Management entrusted the Secretary General, Francisco Longo, with the task of creating and developing the new social debate strategy. In order to achieve this, a team made up of experienced ESADE managers and professors was created to review the background to and evolution of social debate at ESADE, confirming strong quantitative growth as well as the need for a greater focus on strategic alignment. This team created a shared interpretation, defining social debate as 'the exercise of ESADE's social influence, in order to be present in public debate on certain issues, to broadcast messages, encourage and/or facilitate reflection and promote actions and change in the public sphere'.

The objectives of the strategic process and the expected results were then defined as:

1. The social debate model
2. Lines of work
3. Strategic indicators

Step 2: Strategic framework

In defining the new social debate strategy, several meetings were held with key stakeholders (professors, alumni, and corporate units) in order to obtain their input regarding the definition of the strategic framework.

Among the many thought-provoking contributions, emphasis was placed on the importance of the lines of ESADE's mission – education, research, and social debate – highlighting the importance of consistency between them. It was mentioned that: 'People will not understand why research is being carried out in some issues and, at the same time, social debate is dealing with others', adding that for us to focus on social debate, 'there has to be coherence between education and research, and contributions have to be made from a standpoint of diversity'.

Referring to the issue of diversity, comments were made regarding the importance of 'safeguarding freedom of speech'. It was acknowledged that ESADE is plural and that faculty members enjoy academic freedom. 'We shouldn't think in terms of a rigid strategy, but rather in terms of guidelines, which do not exclude plurality.'

Some other reflections were put forward in the form of questions:

- What would be the priorities and how can we give content to the social debate?
- Do we want to have an influence on different subjects or serve as a platform?
- What would we have to do to transform *presence* into *impact*?

The need 'to take social media presence into account' was also mentioned.

Once the strategic framework had been defined, it was presented to various stakeholders (board of trustees, executive committee, professional council, faculty, administrative and services staff) to get feedback. It was reaffirmed at these meetings that **social debate is a responsibility of the first magnitude**, and 'defining priority issues, given that practical success means focusing', was recommended. Research activities once again play a key role in doing this. 'The discussion should be focused on those aspects in which we can demonstrate that we are leaders in research.'

Another of the issues discussed had to do with the definition of indicators. 'How will we know within three years whether the new action plan has been successful? Metrics are very important, we should further explore this and link it to value creation.'

After listening to the various stakeholders, the aims of the social debate strategic framework were outlined, including:

- To focus social debate activities on priorities regarding the contents and approaches used by ESADE to create value in accordance with its mission, values and corporate strategy
- To align ESADE's external activities with the institution and to ensure that they are carried out in a coordinated and coherent manner
- To reinforce ESADE's social influence

Step 3: Action plan

As part of the 2013–14 action plan, and in accordance with the lines that make up the social debate strategic plan, a project focused on a topic of high social impact, job creation, has been set up. The project has a high degree of faculty involvement and includes a research project.

Results and benefits

Progress made in defining the social debate model includes the definition of the contents selection criteria, including consistency with the institutional strategy, relevance of the topic, and connection with the SR-ESADE social responsibility policy.

Moreover, the following general areas have been identified in the definition of the priority social debate contents: changes and keys to addressing new challenges, optimal business model in entrepreneurial and social terms, and society with the highest level of equity and integration.

The role of PRME/sustainability principles

- The PRME initiative has helped enrich our SR Master Plan, as well as enhancing our focus as a business and law school with a serious commitment to social responsibility, ethics, and sustainability.
- PRME provides a global learning network and facilitates the possibility of identifying valuable practices and possible areas for improvement.
- The Sharing Information on Progress (SIP) reports have been a highly valuable tool in taking stock of our progress and have helped us to take into account new challenges and initiatives in our strategic plan.

Reference

Losada, C., Martell, J., and Lozano, J. M. (2011). Responsible business education: Not a question of curriculum but a raison d'être for Business Schools. In Mette Morsing and Alfons Sauquet Rovira (Eds.). *Business Schools and their Contribution to Society*, 2011, pp. 163-174. Sage Publications Ltd. ISBN: 978-0-85702-386-5.

Section 4

Beyond campus introspection

Making impact through networks

20

The Ethos Initiative anti-corruption task force

IEDC-Bled School of Management

Bled, Slovenia

Introduction

The Ethos Initiative's main objective is to lay the foundations for fairer and more sustainable practices of governance in Slovenia through the creation and transfer of knowledge and good practices, taking into account characteristics, needs, and development of the Slovenian social, political, and economic environment. In order to achieve that, the Ethos Initiative has been developing tools and programmes for enhancing knowledge and understanding of the threats corruption presents to integrity and good governance of businesses and has been promoting and facilitating dialogue and debate among relevant stakeholders.

Challenges

Corrupt practices have seemingly become an integral part of many economies, as in Slovenia. Until recently, the impact that corruption had on businesses and society as a whole was never seriously debated and tackled by any institution, not even those promoting responsible management for years. When the Commission for the Prevention of Corruption showed how much the progress of businesses in Slovenia depends on politics and, consequently, how strongly it is creating a less favourable environment for competitiveness and honesty, the focus of attention shifted significantly. The worldwide economic crisis had no doubt contributed integrity and honesty when doing business as an important point on the agenda of numerous events.

Responsible management as a rule entails the promotion of honest, sustainable public–political and corporate practices, for which a common denominator is doing business with integrity. In order to promote such practices and encourage businesses to engage in them, a group of experts have set up a working group within the Global Compact Network Slovenia called the Ethos Initiative. It promotes the implementation of the Ten Principles of the Global Compact, which commits its participants (and calls on all other members of business and society at large) not only to avoid bribery, extortion, and other forms of corruption, but also to develop policies and concrete programmes to address corruption. All in all, the Global Compact calls on all stakeholders to promote 'honest business as a factor of growth and the driver of change'.

Actions taken and results

The Ethos Initiative began in 2010. Its members include representatives of both public and private-sector entities who recognise the importance of empowering businesses with knowledge on the fight against corruption and the enhancement of integrity of both businesses and their employees.

The Ethos Initiative has promoted honest business practices at different events, organised by either the Global Compact Network Slovenia or institutions participating in the Ethos Initiative, with the aim of promoting integrity and zero tolerance of corruption as integral parts of the sustainable and responsible business environment. In order to help businesses to openly promote and implement their core anti-corruption values and principles, different tools and programmes have been developed. They are designed to equip them to be able to identify corrupt practices that are damaging to the quality of their business, progress, and competitiveness as well as to the prosperity of society as a whole.

To date the following have been developed:

- Preparation and promotion of the 'Declaration on Honest Business', introduced to the public with a high-profile business event, 'Fairness as a Source of Sustainable National Competitiveness', in January 2011, attended by 130 top-level executives and decision-makers. The Declaration has since gained 45 signatories (privately owned companies, non-profit organisations and public companies)
- Organisation of a conference by the UNGC Slovenia and the Commission for the Prevention of Corruption on 'Corrupt Practices in Business Environment' for privately owned companies
- A round table organised by the Global Compact Network Slovenia, the Ekvilib Institute and the Managers Association of Slovenia on 'Honest Business as a Factor of Growth and the Driver of Change' in December 2011
- A conference organised by the UNGC Slovenia and the Commission for the Prevention of Corruption on 'Identify the Corruption Risks' in November 2012
- A discussion organised by the Commission for the Prevention of Corruption and the Chamber of Commerce and Industry of Slovenia on the 'Impact of Corruption on the Slovenian Economy' in 2013
- Presentation of the Ethos Initiative and its objectives at the international conference 'Social Responsibility and Current Challenges 2013', organised by the Institute for the Development of Social Responsibility (IRDO)

Main goals of the Ethos Initiative for the future are:

- To raise awareness and understanding on the importance of integrity and honest business in wider society, including entities of the public and private sector
- To educate on anti-corruption practices and honest business
- To impact policy-making and guidelines on integrity and honest business at the state level as well as at the level of different organisations sharing common business interests
- To develop a certificate for integrity plans and/or anti-corruption compliance programmes and to issue them

These goals will be realised through:

- Active participation at and organisation of events, publication of expert papers, and organisation of training and workshops for relevant stakeholders, including youth
- Regular update of the Ethos Initiative website
- Preparation of news for the signatories of the declaration and members of Global Compact Network Slovenia,
- Preparation of drafts and proposals for policies and guidelines in the area of honest business and affecting different bodies and interest groups
- Preparation and implementation of a programme for certifying and maintaining requirements for the certificate for integrity plans and/or anti-corruption compliance programmes

The Ethos Initiative is committed to making the most of circumstances in which businesses are aware that their progress, reputation, and even existence are at stake and call for immediate (re)action from managers and the economy. Such initiatives are becoming part of responsible management, a reaction to the current situation in the economy and society as a whole.

The mission of the project is to establish mechanisms, processes, and know-how with which the economy would be able to proactively and, through its own initiative (without pressure from repressive organs), fight corruption, and increase compliance to ethical and legal norms.

The role of PRME/sustainability principles

- Taking the dialogue a step further – into action
- Participation of very different stakeholders gives us an unbiased view of the playing-field
- Multisectoral structure facilitates design of sustainable tools for all players

21

Levelling the playing field in the electric power transmission industry in Argentina

IAE Business School Universidad Austral

Pilar, Buenos Aires, Argentina

Introduction

The Center for Governance and Transparency at IAE Business School in Argentina undertook the facilitator role in fostering the implementation of a collective action agreement among companies in the local electric power transmission industry in order to address integrity, regulatory, and competition problems. With the ongoing development and growth of the initiative, the established partnership among the main players in the sector seeks to have a lasting impact in the way business is done in this sector.

Challenges

Over the years, the electric power transmission industry in Argentina became a complex sector where companies often faced regulatory, fair competition, and integrity challenges. Usually, these problems were dealt with individually or through their respective industry associations but frequently these concerns were not adequately channelled or managed, creating an understandable sense of frustration. Simultaneously, a lack of trust and understanding of business practices and fairness among some players – in particular, multinational enterprises (MNEs) and small local companies – had to be overcome.

Actions taken

In late 2011, one of the main industry players approached the Center for Governance and Transparency in order to explore the possibility of starting some sort of partnership with other competitors whom they regarded as sharing, to some extent, the same concerns about integrity problems. The Center accepted the challenge, extending an invitation to attend a first exploratory meeting with the CEOs of the five main companies present in the sector, which accounted for a sizeable chunk of the market, big and small MNEs, and a local company. There was consensus among companies present that some sort of joint action was needed if things were to change. The Center made the proposition of negotiating and signing a collective action agreement in the form of a Principles-based Initiative. The companies accepted the challenge and began examining the main issues and problems faced by their sector. In a second step, priorities were established and behavioural standards discussed and agreed on, which were then included in the collective action. Based on those discussions, they signed an agreement in June 2012 in regard to ten standards:

1. Conducting their business operations in a fair, honest, transparent manner, strictly abiding by all current Argentine laws, as well as the principles laid out by the UN Convention Against Corruption and the Inter-American Convention Against Corruption
2. Refraining from paying any kind of bribe (direct or indirect bribery)
3. Refusing to accept bribes or to let others accept bribes on their behalf

4. Avoiding bid tampering or engaging in any form of bid or technical, commercial, and/or financial specification tampering
5. Refraining from making local contributions to political campaigns
6. Maintaining clear, transparent sponsoring, giving and charitable contribution policies, recording all donations accurately in their financial statements
7. Maintaining or establishing effective internal processes to prevent direct or indirect bribery
8. Ensuring that their employees, business partners, and third parties embrace these principles, providing adequate training to that end
9. Trying to avoid doing business with others who do not abide by these principles or who may jeopardise these companies' reputations
10. Actively promoting transparency in their industry by engaging in coordinated communication and training efforts to disseminate this collective action agreement, so that others become aware of its provisions and align their behaviour with them

Along with the ten standards, an Ethics Committee was set up to serve as a forum for disputes arising from the execution of this Principle-Based Initiative and as a platform for exchanging and sharing good practices. The Ethics Committee is empowered to sanction any member that infringes the collective action principles.

The Center for Governance and Transparency, in its role as facilitator, agreed to meet the signing members at least twice a year to review the Initiative's progress and to discuss any developments arising from its execution or future changes.

Results and benefits

The Center produced a press release to inform the media and the general public about the scope and objectives of the collective action, whereas companies communicated internally to their employees the signature of the agreement through their intranets and made it public through their respective websites and online portals. On top of that, they sent messages to suppliers, clients, etc. Both company employees and value-chain actors received the news positively.

In the meantime, one new participant has joined the initiative. Other potential members are currently being considered to be part of the agreement. Based on the success of the agreement and its positive repercussions, a further extension is being examined.

Whereas the positive reception of the initiative and its growth in the form of new members attest to its practical impact, the initiative has another important and lasting effect: it creates and progressively increases trust among participating companies, creating a community of like-minded 'partners'. If, during the first steps, there were concerns and, to some extent, mistrust about the different sizes and business styles of the participating members (e.g. multinationals versus national companies, large versus medium/small enterprises, etc.), ongoing discussions allow a more in-depth knowledge of the values and principles of the competitors, understanding the extent to which they share the same integrity problems.

The role of PRME/sustainability principles

- Corruption and integrity problems can be tackled effectively through partnership between committed business actors
- Collective action partnerships have a dynamic, open-ended nature, allowing an ongoing and ever-growing involvement of additional stakeholders and interested parties
- Educational institutions can play a key role in facilitating collective actions: they are regarded as neutral by business actors and can effectively coordinate the necessary steps that lead to the signature of such an agreement

22

Empowering African business schools: The 39 Country Initiative

Ivey Business School Western University

London, Ontario, Canada

Introduction

The Ivey Business School at Western University initiated the 39 Country Initiative in 2010. The 39 Country Initiative looks to assist poverty-reduction efforts by improving the quality of business education in the world's 39 least developed countries, of which 32 are in Africa. This case story discusses the school's efforts in (a) developing the capabilities of university students in the world's poorest countries, (b) allowing its own students to learn from and contribute to the learning of their counterparts in those countries, and (c) making educational materials available – including books, articles, cases, and teaching notes – to assist in the development of capable and responsible future managers and leaders.

Challenges

Economic growth leads to the expansion of businesses, thereby calling for relevant managerial skills. A key group that assists with developing such expertise is business schools. However, most African business schools are not yet able to properly play such a role, with limited access to teaching materials, outdated facilities, or not enough qualified instructors. The implications of such limited capacity will become even more pressing with the continent's increasing integration into the dynamic and complex global economy.

To this end, a three-pronged strategy was formulated to help business schools in those countries play more active roles in producing well-trained and responsible management professionals able to work in the increasingly complex business environment. The 39 Country Initiative addresses three critical challenges: (a) the lack of current teaching material, (b) the insufficient quantity of books and other reference materials available, and (3) the limited numbers and qualifications of faculty at business schools in the target countries.

Actions taken and results

In regards to the lack of current teaching material, considerable progress has already been made. Ivey Publishing, the second largest producer and distributor of case studies, allows faculty in the eligible countries free access to its cases, technical notes, and articles, comprising nearly 50,000 pages of proprietary content. To date, over 1,150 professors and their students from the 32 eligible African countries have registered for this opportunity. Not only does this access allow the faculty at hundreds of African universities to draw on a huge collection of high-quality current material, it also opens up the opportunity for them to apply the case-based teaching method, which has proved relevant and suitable for business education.

Partnering with business schools in Africa, Ivey also developed a course in which its senior undergraduate and MBA students visit select business schools in Africa to teach short, introductory case-based courses and develop understanding of the African business environment. In addition, professor-to-professor case-teaching workshops have been offered at various African business schools to illustrate the proper use of cases. Through these efforts, Ivey has demonstrated its commitment to empowering business schools in Africa and their faculty members.

Cognisant of the acute shortages of current, hard-copy teaching materials, Ivey has also embarked on an effort to collect books, journals, cases, course packs, and readings and ship them to business schools in the 39 countries. To this end, many Ivey faculty and students and the bookstore at Western University in London, Ontario, have agreed to donate their surplus and used books. As a result, a huge collection of content has been received and preparations are underway to make an initial container shipment to Addis Ababa University School of Commerce. Similar efforts are afoot to encourage business schools at other universities in North America and Western Europe to collect teaching materials for separate universities in Africa.

While all of these activities require effort, time, and cost on the part of Ivey, the initiative allows Ivey the opportunity to live its vision of being an agent of positive change. It also affords Ivey the opportunity to make truly meaningful contributions by assisting in preparing future African managers and leaders for the challenges and opportunities ahead. More importantly, it enables African business schools to play active roles in building their respective economies by producing well-trained and responsible management professionals who contribute to their society by balancing economic, social, and environmental priorities.

23

More women on boards for decision quality

Sabanci University School of Management

Istanbul, Turkey

Introduction

A small number of family-owned conglomerates control a large part of Turkey's economy through largely male and affiliated boards. This structure has significant economic and social consequences not only for women, investors, and employees, but also for the wider society. The Independent Women Directors (IWD) Project was initiated by Sabanci University School of Management through its Corporate Governance Forum, a research and advocacy centre, in partnership with Egon Zehnder International, an international executive search firm, and the Swedish Consulate in Istanbul to address this issue.

IWD's purpose is to create awareness on the benefits of board diversity, develop and maintain a database of qualified women in cooperation with business schools, and match the women in the database with companies wishing to nominate women to their boards. Since women empowerment has been identified as one of the Turkish government's strategic priorities, the IWD Project has found a fertile ground to initiate a collaboration between the listed companies, the regulator, the stock exchange, various women-led initiatives, and researchers in order to improve the gender balance at the top of business organisations. The objective of the project is to have no listed companies without a woman director by 2015.

The project is a case demonstrating how universities can use their credibility, their global network, and their knowledge and capabilities to influence corporate agendas, promote a dialogue between different stakeholders on challenging issues, and facilitate collaborative action by providing intellectual leadership and scientific input.

Challenges

Our studies show that female representation at the board level is very low in Turkey, with only 49 professional female board members in 2010 in the top 100 listed companies, yet educated women face little discrimination in entering the workforce and pursuit of a professional career is supported by social structures and norms. The IWD project was designed in order to bring about a fundamental shift in the gender balance in these positions of influence so that men and women in Turkey can have an equal voice in economic decisions.

A recent regulatory reform in the governance of Turkish corporations presented an opportunity to accelerate and support gender equality at the top of Turkish corporations. According to amendments to the Corporate Governance Principles issued by the capital markets regulator in 2012, companies are required to have at least one woman on their boards, while one-third of the directors must be independent. The provision related to the presence of women is a recommendation in line with the approach of 'comply or explain'; firms that do not comply with the principle must explain the reasons in their mandatory annual compliance reports; however, the independence requirement is mandatory. The 2012 general assemblies showed that most of the independent member positions were filled by men, with a few exceptions, while the recommended quotas for women have been disregarded.

This bias towards men in the nomination of independent directors reduced the percentage of women directors from 12 per cent to 11 per cent. The arguments provided by the companies that did not comply with the recommendation of having at least one woman director were largely based on their perceived lack of suitable women.

Based on the above, in collaboration with our business school alumni network, we decided to develop a methodology for (1) building a database of female candidates with strong backgrounds who are 'board ready', and (2) developing a methodology to match specific company needs with the female candidates and hence challenge the notion that there are not enough women who can serve as independent directors on the boards of Turkish corporations.

The first challenge was to convince women to apply to be a part of the database, as this could have been interpreted as looking for jobs. The second challenge was to convince the companies that agree on the benefits of diversity to act now rather than later. Since appointment of a woman director would under many circumstances mean asking a male independent director to step down, and this is not a straightforward transaction in a country such as Turkey where relationships matter, we focused on giving priority to women for newly established independent director positions. The third challenge was the existing policies of business groups not to allow their executives, male or female, to sit on the boards of non-group companies as independent directors. The last challenge was convincing the faculty to allocate time and effort to a non-academic activity.

Actions taken

We have overcome some of the challenges by working together with a professional executive search firm, establishing an advisory board consisting of women and men who are well known and respected in the business world, engaging with journalists and commentators who could promote the project, making references to scientific research about the reasons behind the 'glass ceiling' and the benefits of diversity, organising panel discussions, and presenting role models. We are in the process of writing a series of white papers, which will discuss some of the common practices in Turkey such as staggered boards, the benefits of allowing executive directors to sit on other boards, and so on.

We have also analysed existing director networks to identify 'friends' or 'ambassadors' of the project who can penetrate these networks and promote the project. Our affiliation with the Global Board Ready Women Project helped us to convince some of the high-profile executive women to agree to be on the IWD database, with the prospect of visibility in the international directors market.

The support from the faculty was easily achieved since Sabanci School of Management has one of the few female Deans in Turkey who also participated in the Advisory Board of the project.

The project is planned in five main phases:

- **Phase 1:** Methodology development for creating a universe of qualified women candidates for corporate boards
- **Phase 2:** Data collection based on the methodology developed in Phase 1
- **Phase 3:** Methodology development for matching candidates with companies based on company characteristics and candidates' skills and background
- **Phase 4:** Utilisation of the database and methodology through pilot implementation for listed companies in Turkey, and facilitating recruitment of independent women candidates in company boards
- **Phase 5:** Strategy development to ensure future use and enhancement of a women director database to facilitate development of a network of women directors, which would contribute to the improvement of working conditions for women through jointly undertaken programmes, campaigns, and actions

Results and benefits

- As of May 2013, Phases 1, 2, and 3 are complete with a resulting database of 250 qualified women
- This was achieved with the help of a 20-member Advisory Board consisting of high-profile representatives from business associations, media, the capital market regulator, and senior woman directors
- All the listed companies were informed about the existence of the database
- Women in the IWD database were invited by Bourse Istanbul to ring the opening bell of the trading session on 8 March, International Women's Day
- A committee has been established to lobby for changing the soft approach to board gender diversity to a mandatory ruling
- Five companies were targeted as pilot companies. As a result, four women have been appointed to the board of four companies that previously had all male boards. A number of companies with staggered boards expressed their intention to work with the IWD project next year

Project activities such as round tables, press conferences, panels, and conferences motivated professional women to be more vocal about the 'glass ceiling' and to support each other. A regulatory committee has been established within the Advisory Board to develop a proposal to change the diversity regulation from a recommendation to a mandatory requirement of at least one independent woman director and increase the recommended level of gender diversity.

A spin-off of the IWD project is 'Business Against Domestic Violence' which will be launched in the third quarter of 2013 to mobilise woman directors to develop best practices to protect their female employees from domestic violence, a serious problem in Turkey. We should expect improvements in working conditions of women employed at all levels and increased sensitivity to women's rights issues, as women become represented at the board level. As we move forward, wider societal impacts are expected, since women are more sensitive to stakeholder issues.

The role of PRME/sustainability principles

PRME has provided a basis and justification for the project to be homed at a business school.

- Principle 4 encouraged us to investigate the effect of board diversity on corporate performance and also develop a normative position based on the role of women's empowerment in sustainable development
- Principle 5 inspired us to engage with businesses as a facilitator and enabler of change towards better functioning and more diverse boards
- Principle 6 is what we do best on a continuous basis; the mission of our university is a sound foundation and great encouragement for our community outreach projects

24 *Forming local leaders: Expanding PRME performance in Brazil*

ISAE/FGV
Curitiba, Paraná, Brazil

Introduction

ISAE (Instituto Superior de Administração e Economia – the Higher Institute of Administration and Economics) is a business school located in the south of Brazil that enrols more than 5,000 students a year in post-graduate courses. Since 1996, ISAE has operated in an innovative and cross-sectional way, seeking to mobilise and help the market, in respect to responsible practices that generate sustainable development.

This case story presents a strategy for expansion and consolidation of the PRME in Brazil, with the objective of strengthening the sustainability movement in the country by training local leaders and integrating the network as a whole. The intention of this work is to awaken academic institutions and corporate universities in Brazil to the new role played by education in tackling the challenges of sustainability.

ISAE assumed this mobilisation since joined PRME in 2008, having contributed to the institutionalisation of the PRME Chapter Brazil and to the improvement of the Brazilian network as a whole. This improvement in performance happens when signatory institutions have access to contacts, study groups, news, data, and materials such as case studies and researches, and engage in rich benchmarking of practices and policies related to education for sustainability.

Challenges

When taking up the challenge of participating in the creation of PRME in 2006, ISAE strengthened its actions in the area of education for sustainability, having this new scope as the main guide to its management. Thus, ISAE has gone through all the steps in the process of changing its mental model – understanding the concepts, internalising the values of sustainability in the school's strategy and management, involving and training the various publics, and including these contents in the whole student experience through its exclusive educational method called Perspectivaction. ISAE fulfilled the various stages of implementation of the PRME, experiencing difficulties and reaping rewards.

However, in 2011, ISAE faced one of the biggest challenges in the performance of a PRME signatory school – disseminating the Principles of PRME and the Global Compact in other regions of the country. It is important to stress that the decision to take this new step was only possible after ISAE had gone through the previous steps in implementing the Principles, thus having the necessary maturity to engage other institutions and seeking to strengthen and extend the network in such a large country as Brazil.

Actions taken and results

By promoting the International Seminar on Education for Sustainability, which was held in Curitiba (Paraná state) in September 2011, ISAE took the initial step in its strategy to mobilise other institutions in the region. The event was a success, and the Brazilian network of PRME signatories more than doubled (from 9 to 19 institutions). To assure quality to the signatories, the ISAE began to gather this new group of institutions for frequent workshops. In these workshops, veteran signatories contribute to the understanding and implementation of the principles, giving valuable advice and tips with the experience of those who have already gone through several steps in the implementation process.

Thus, in these three years, ISAE took part in the mobilisation of events and actions in many Brazilian capitals, such as São Paulo, Brasília, Rio de Janeiro, Porto Alegre, Belo Horizonte, and Curitiba (where ISAE is located). There were also numerous mobilisations in favour of the PRME and the Global Compact in Paraná, which were held in partnership with the Federation of Industries of the State of Paraná. The most recent action brought more than 20 participants to the Global Compact.

In addition to this regional action, ISAE has also started to act in the northern and north-eastern regions of Brazil. With the aim of decentralising the sustainability movement in the country, ISAE went to the state of Ceará to visit nearly 12 academic institutions, introducing the Principles and the importance of taking part in an initiative that supports the formation of responsible leaders. Invited by the Federation of Industries of the State of Ceará (FIEC), the Institute has also promoted a lecture on responsible leaders for more than 200 entrepreneurs and educators from the capital city Fortaleza and the metropolitan region.

This relationship with FIEC is a highlight within the Brazilian strategy for consolidating the Principles. In the case of Ceará, the institution will be the major vector to help develop the work, without which the efforts might die due to lack of continuity. Developing local leaders in alignment with the Principles will have positive results, ensuring that the contacted institutions also establish a relationship for a rich exchange of information in the quest to improve the performance of the group as a whole. Moving forward, ISAE intends to visit other regions in Brazil and promote an annual event with the PRME Chapter Brazil, while seeking the consolidation and expansion of sustainability principles in Brazil by developing institutions and more prepared leaders to deal with the challenges of sustainability.

Section 5

Beyond education-only
Harnessing research and publication

25

Social science student community engagement

Glasgow Caledonian University

Glasgow, Scotland, United Kingdom

Introduction

This case is about developing an engaged curriculum within social sciences, which are not generally associated with business engagement and perhaps even less so in the context of teaching. This case story reports on the impact of an innovative teaching approach: an accredited module at Glasgow Caledonian University – Community Links – that supports social science students in applying their knowledge and skills acquired in the academy through engagement with community, voluntary, and statutory organisations.

Challenges

The value of social sciences in the context of business is often overlooked. Furthermore, social science students often struggle to make links between the learning in the academy and its application in the wider social and work context.

The Community Links module was developed using staff research and consultancy networks to identify a number of community, voluntary, and statutory organisations that had small projects that they were keen to have undertaken but lacked the funds, the time, or the knowledge to do so. This provided a unique opportunity for students to be involved in projects that would be mutually beneficial to the university, the student, and the host organisation.

Actions taken

The module provides a supportive and structured approach for students to apply their academic knowledge and learn how to plan and carry out research activities, understand the relevance of specific social issues within their host organisation, demonstrate and apply their knowledge and understanding to that specified social issue, reflect on their experience of working within an outside agency, and draw conclusions about the role of, and the process of undertaking, research. Assessment includes a short account of the agency's work, a research plan, the research output, their research diary, and an assessment from the host organisation.

Good partnerships have been established with a number of organisations such as Strathclyde Police,[1] Greater Glasgow and Clyde National Health Board, SACRO,[2] Poverty Alliance, Rape Crisis, and Glasgow Women's Library. Annually they identify a piece of research they would like done within the broad field of social and criminal justice issues, or social history.

The key to the success of this module is two-fold: the research is of value to the organisation, and the interests of the students can be matched with the requirements of the organisation's proposals.

Brief synopses of two projects are offered here with comments from the supporting organisations and the student researchers,

---

1   Since 1 April 2013, the eight Scottish police forces combined to become one national force to be known as Police Scotland.
2   SACRO: Safeguarding Communities – Reducing Offending. SACRO aims to promote community safety across Scotland through providing high-quality services to reduce conflict and offending.

which exemplify how this module meets the needs of all parties and is in line with the Principles of PRME.

Project 1

Organisation: Unite the Union

The project: Project undertaken in Trimester 2, 2012: to conduct research with young people to enhance Unite the Union's knowledge and understanding of the issues faced by young people entering the job market for the first time or seeking employment and how the union could support them in making that transition.

Output: A written report and a video[3]

The student's view: 'Community Links has given me an insight into the role of a researcher and confidence in my abilities to conduct research by enabling me to apply my knowledge gained in the academy to real-life circumstances. It has also enhanced my knowledge of the Trade Union movement and of young people's experiences of unemployment and the issues they face. The module provides opportunities unavailable otherwise, equipped me with practical research experience, enhanced computer skills, and references for my CV.'

The organisation's view: 'The research outputs have provided a deeper and more nuanced understanding of the issues faced by young people. The documentary and podcast are on the website and the written report will also be posted online.'

This student also attended Unite the Union's annual Conference in London to present the findings from her research to a wider audience.

Project 2

Organisation: Strathclyde Police

The project: Project undertaken in Trimester 2, 2011: to undertake qualitative research into the issues of reporting domestic abuse in adolescents' relationships.

---

3   http://www.youtube.com/watch?v=I8ysqfy9I5U

Output: An interesting and thought-provoking report.

The student's view: 'Community Links has developed my transferrable skills, particularly oral and written communication, referencing and research skills including research design and impartiality. One of the main benefits of Community Links is working with an organisation external to the university where expectations were found to be higher. It also encourages independent learning in a supportive environment and encourages you to take responsibility for completing the project within the set timescales.'

The organisation's view: 'The report is useful to us as it provides an insight into our understanding (or lack thereof) of domestic abuse and potential barriers to reporting identified by young people. It will be used to inform targeting of resources in respect of media campaigns to (hopefully) positively impact on the number of domestic abuse reports received from young people.'

Results and benefits

The research reports/outputs compiled by the students have been used in a number of submissions to the Scottish Government and Funding Councils in support of bids by statutory, community, and voluntary organisations to apply for funding for various reasons.

Furthermore, students report that it greatly enhances their organisational skills, particularly for entering the workplace, as it is, they say, an excellent module to have on their CV-employers are impressed by the students' achievements. Some students have been offered employment with the agencies for which they carried out the research and it has forged stronger links and closer partnership working between some community groups and the academy for research, networking, and information exchange, and involvement in learning and teaching.

The role of PRME/sustainability principles

This module fits with a number of the Principles of the PRME, particularly those that have an aim to facilitate and support student community engagement and student capabilities. For example, in:

- Incorporating into our academic activities and curricula the values of global social responsibility
- Creating educational frameworks, materials, processes, and environments that enable effective learning experiences
- Engaging in conceptual and empirical research that advances our understanding about the role, dynamics, and impact of corporations in the creation of sustainable social, environmental, and economic value
- Educating students, business, government, consumers, media, civil society organisations, and other interested groups and stakeholders on critical issues related to global social responsibility and sustainability

26

Researching poverty alleviation through third-sector initiatives in Scotland

Yunus Centre for Social Business and Health
Glasgow Caledonian University

Glasgow, Scotland, United Kingdom

Introduction

Reinforcing its commitment to the 'common weal' (the common good), Glasgow Caledonian University (GCU) established the Yunus Centre for Social Business and Health in 2010. The aim of the Yunus Centre is to develop and support social action to meet major societal challenges and to carry out research to continuously improve the value of such action.

Our hope is that GCU's Yunus Centre provides a model for Principle 4 (Research) of the PRME within 'modern' universities, creating a socially impactful area of academic endeavour in line with its mission and achieved through enabling:

1. The world's first centre of excellence in the field of social business and health
2. Comprehensive frameworks of outcomes and instruments for evaluating future social business innovation from perspectives of social cohesion, health and well-being
3. A compelling evidence base for social business as a health and well-being intervention, through quantitative and qualitative methods of enquiry
4. Development of multidisciplinary research capacity in an area of major and growing international importance

Social business and health is a subject for our time, reflecting the need to think and act differently at this key juncture in our history, aspiring to evidence-based sustainable well-being for all.

Thus, through the development of new conceptual frameworks and evaluating the impacts of new ways of 'doing business' this initiative embodies the spirit of Principle 4 (Research). At the same time, Principle 6 (Dialogue) is also key to this work, given that it involves dialogue and collaboration with multiple stakeholders.

Challenges

By any standards, the UK has world-class health services; yet health inequalities continue to grow. This is one aspect of wider social inequality, not least in terms of income, reflected more widely in Europe and disproportionately in some regions. One quarter of Glasgow's citizens are defined as deprived, with life-expectancy gaps, shown in the work of Sir Michael Marmot,[1] of up to 28 years between richest and poorest.

Public health initiatives focusing on individual risk factors, such as diet or exercise, need to be complemented by interventions acting further back along the chain of causality. If low income, societal exclusion and hopelessness kill people prematurely, we need to work on such 'causes of the causes' through more holistic interventions that come from communities themselves. These might be enhanced via encouragement of self-help and change from a culture of dependency. This has led to a convergence of thinking about the need for entities, such as **social businesses**, that focus on people and communities as assets to be built upon,

---

[1]   WHO Report on Health Inequalities, written by a Commission chaired by Sir Michael Marmot; http://www.who.int/social_determinants/thecommission/finalreport/about_csdh/en/index.html

with solutions coming largely from them rather than imposed from outside. This requires parallel development of approaches to measuring 'economic success', accounting for broader aspects of well-being.[2]

Actions taken

Social business has existed in various forms since the 18th century, but has not been viewed as or evaluated as a public health intervention. Despite recent focus on social business as an alternative provider of health services, researchers in GCU's Yunus Centre are thinking of it in a much wider and more exciting role; acting on broader and structural determinants of health. Lying outside traditional service-focused arenas, social businesses are characterised by having a social (not profit-led) mission and a trading function, with no share ownership or dividends paid in the event of surplus. Any surplus is 'ploughed back' into the community served in line with the mission. In addressing conditions of society's most vulnerable, almost all social businesses could claim to act on 'upstream' determinants of health.

This cutting-edge thinking matches the European Commission's placement of social innovation at the heart of its vision for Europe 2020 and the World Health Organization's promotion of assets-based approaches to health. Bringing together expressed requirements to address needs and measure success differently, and working across the Glasgow School for Business and Society and GCU's School of Health and Life Sciences, GCU's Yunus Centre is developing a new scientific interface, conceptualising and evidencing 'social business as a public health and well-being intervention'.

2   See New Economics Foundation at www.neweconomics.org.

Results and benefits

Since its creation in 2010, the work of GCU's Yunus Centre has gained international recognition, creating the social actions and accompanying research environment for new pathways to health and well-being to thrive. Major examples are:

- Establishment and evaluation of Grameen Caledonian College of Nursing in Bangladesh, officially opened by HRH the Princess Royal in March 2011. This social enterprise addresses serious social needs and provides professional training to the disadvantaged.
- Facilitating the partnership of Grameen and Tesco Banks to bring affordable microcredit for entrepreneurship to the most deprived parts of the UK.
- Establishment of an exciting and young cadre of academic staff and postgraduate researchers. Their task is to develop evaluation frameworks of a longitudinal mixed-method nature, permitting as rigorous attribution of outcomes to social business innovations as is possible. So far, funding has been captured from the Medical Research Council and the National Institute for Health Research (NIHR) as well as national and international donors – the Church of Scotland, Santander Bank, and the Nike Foundation.
- Building potential for cross-cultural comparisons, not only involving lower-income countries but through GCU's establishment of a campus in New York City and growing links with the State University of New York.

The role of PRME/sustainability principles

- This research advances our understanding about the role, dynamics, and impact of social business in the creation of sustainable social and economic value

- The collaborative approach extends our knowledge of the challenges in meeting social and economic responsibilities and promotes dialogue to explore effective approaches to meeting these challenges

27 *Empowering responsible management education through book publishing*

Center for Responsible Management Education

Berlin, Germany, and Manchester, England, United Kingdom

Introduction

The Center for Responsible Management Education (CRME) was founded as a university-independent organisation with the mission of supporting responsible management education and empowering responsible managers. CRME recognised the lack of textbooks in responsible management education and, in response, published graduate and undergraduate textbooks and established a 'PRME Book Collection'.

Challenges

Many business schools worldwide have begun to integrate topics related to responsible management into their curricula, which were initiated before the foundation of PRME and continue with the Principles. Those courses were and mostly still are conducted from an organisational-level perspective, exhibiting typical course titles such as business and society, corporate social responsibility, business ethics, or sustainable business. While those courses are an important development forward, few courses exist that specifically approach the managerial level. CRME made its *raison d'être* to support educators and academic institutions in the design of educational activities, courses, and programmes. These educators and institutions would then empower responsible managers in their day-to-day activities on a managerial level. The immediate challenge to address before achieving this goal was the dearth of educational materials for responsible management education.

Actions taken

CRME first focused on establishing contacts with publishing houses that were interested in contracting books related to responsible management education. Communication with educators, practitioners, publishers, and the PRME Secretariat resulted in four types of book that were needed: an undergraduate-level textbook, a graduate-level textbook, a secondary textbook bringing PRME aspects into mainstream business courses, and guides for educators and responsible management practitioners. As a consequence, the following three publication projects were initiated through a collaborative multi-stakeholder model involving educators, academics, and practitioners:

- **Graduate-level textbook:** The graduate textbook titled 'Principles of Responsible Management' will be published in autumn 2013 through the publisher Cengage. The book is most adequate for business students at the graduate level. Chapters cover context and theory of management, the concepts of sustainability, responsibility and ethics, and how they are applied throughout mainstream business functions, from accounting to strategy.
- **Undergraduate-level textbook:** 'Responsible Business: Theory, Practice, Change' will be published in an interactive e-book format in summer 2013. The book content is appropriate for undergraduate and multidisciplinary courses. The interactive e-book format is designed to be

especially attractive for younger, Internet-native students and allows for global availability at a very accessible price.

- **PRME Book Collection:** The PRME Book Collection is a series of books centred on the publication of secondary PRME-related textbooks and guides for educators and practitioners of responsible management through the publisher Business Expert Press.

Results and benefits

By May 2013, these activities had provided publication opportunities to more than 100 educators, academics, and practitioners. The publications allowed interdisciplinary knowledge creation and theory–practice transfer between academics and practitioners. The PRME Book Collection had signed 14 books on responsible management education for publication, out of which four were already published.

Even before its official publication in autumn 2013, the graduate textbook had been well received. Five out of six reviewers stated they would probably adopt the book. Positive points they highlighted included the conceptual rigour, practical application, and strong chapter structure. More than a dozen academic institutions had made firm commitments to use 'Principles of Responsible Management Education' for their courses, and the book has been pilot tested at five universities. The book features contributions from over 50 topic experts, among them pioneers such as John Elkington, Edward Freeman, and Philip Kotler.

The powerful network of educators, authors, and practitioners that formed during the publishing process enabled CRME to support academic institutions in the design and implementation of their responsible management education activities. By May 2013, projects with different partner institutions globally included the establishment of a responsible management executive education programme, the development of a 'Responsible MBA', web-based coaching of responsible management practitioners, and the design and coordination of e-learning modules in responsible management. These activities involved more than 25 responsible management experts on a regular basis.

The role of PRME/sustainability principles

- The Principles have provided crucial guidance for the work process
- The networks of the PRME have proven to be a highly participative community of practice, greatly contributing to the establishment of high-quality publications
- The PRME Secretariat was highly supportive in the publication process, with Jonas Haertle, Head, having contributed to two publications
- PRME, as a brand, has helped to strengthen initial trust of CRME projects among publishers and contributors

Appendices

Appendix 1: The Six Principles of the Principles for Responsible Management Education

As institutions of higher education involved in the development of current and future managers we declare our willingness to progress in the implementation, within our institution, of the following Principles, starting with those that are more relevant to our capacities and mission. We will report on progress to all our stakeholders and exchange effective practices related to these principles with other academic institutions:

Principle 1

Purpose: We will develop the capabilities of students to be future generators of sustainable value for business and society at large and to work for an inclusive and sustainable global economy.

Principle 2

Values: We will incorporate into our academic activities and curricula the values of global social responsibility as portrayed in international initiatives such as the United Nations Global Compact.

Principle 3

Method: We will create educational frameworks, materials, processes and environments that enable effective learning experiences for responsible leadership.

Principle 4

Research: We will engage in conceptual and empirical research that advances our understanding about the role, dynamics, and impact of corporations in the creation of sustainable social, environmental and economic value.

Principle 5

Partnership: We will interact with managers of business corporations to extend our knowledge of their challenges in meeting social and environmental responsibilities and to explore jointly effective approaches to meeting these challenges.

Principle 6

Dialogue: We will facilitate and support dialogue and debate among educators, students, business, government, consumers, media, civil society organisations and other interested groups and stakeholders on critical issues related to global social responsibility and sustainability.

We understand that our own organisational practices should serve as an example of the values and attitudes we convey to our students.

Appendix 2: The Ten Principles of the United Nations Global Compact

The United Nations Global Compact's Ten Principles in the areas of human rights, labour, the environment, and anti-corruption enjoy universal consensus and are derived from:

- The Universal Declaration of Human Rights
- The International Labour Organization's Declaration on Fundamental Principles and Rights at Work
- The Rio Declaration on Environment and Development
- The United Nations Convention Against Corruption

The UN Global Compact asks companies to embrace, support, and enact, within their sphere of influence, a set of core values in the areas of human rights, labour standards, the environment, and anti-corruption:

Human Rights

- Principle 1: Businesses should support and respect the protection of internationally proclaimed human rights; and
- Principle 2: make sure that they are not complicit in human rights abuses.

Labour

- Principle 3: Businesses should uphold the freedom of association and the effective recognition of the right to collective bargaining;
- Principle 4: the elimination of all forms of forced and compulsory labour;
- Principle 5: the effective abolition of child labour; and
- Principle 6: the elimination of discrimination in respect of employment and occupation.

Environment

- Principle 7: Businesses should support a precautionary approach to environmental challenges;
- Principle 8: undertake initiatives to promote greater environmental responsibility; and
- Principle 9: encourage the development and diffusion of environmentally friendly technologies.

Anti-Corruption

- Principle 10: Businesses should work against corruption in all its forms, including extortion and bribery.

Appendix 3:
Co-editor biographies

The PRME Secretariat would like to extend special thanks to the co-editors of this second edition:

Merrill Csuri is Manager of the PRME Secretariat and served as project manager for both the first and second editions of the Guide.

Oliver Laasch is founder of the Center for Responsible Management Education (CRME) and a Marie Curie Research Fellow at the University of Manchester. He is editor of the Business Expert Press PRME Book Collection and author of the PRME textbook *Principles of Responsible Management: Global Sustainability, Responsibility, Ethics.*

F. Byron (Ron) Nahser is Senior Wicklander Fellow; Director, Urban Sustainable Management Program, Institute for Business and Professional Ethics, Driehaus College of Business, DePaul University. Provost Emeritus, Presidio Graduate School. Author of Learning to Read the Signs (2nd edition), published as part of the GSE Research and Greenleaf Publishing PRME Book Series.

Giselle Weybrecht is author of The Sustainable MBA: The Manager's Guide to Green Business and a writer, speaker, lecturer and consultant on sustainability issues within management education. She also writes the PRiMEtime blog, a joint initiative with the PRME Secretariat.

The PRME Secretariat and the co-editors of this second edition would like to extend special thanks to the co-editors of the first edition: Manuel Escudero, Laura Albareda, Jose M. Alcaraz, Giselle Weybrecht, and Merrill Csuri, as well as the host of the 2013 PRME Summit, CEEMAN, namely: Danica Purg, Milenko Gudić, and Špela Horjak, and the developers of the Summit programme and materials, including: Anthony Buono, Jean-Christophe Carteron, Matthew Gitsham, Jonathan Gosling, Jonas Haertle, Satoshi Miura, Ron Nahser, and Nadya Zhexembayeva.

Appendix 4: Case story contributors and reviewers

We would like to thank all contributors and reviewers of the case stories included in this Guide who, through their work, make PRME a thriving learning community.

- **Ahmed M. Abdel-Meguid**, American University in Cairo School of Business, Egypt
- **Melsa Ararat**, Independent Women Directors Project, Sabanci University School of Management, Turkey
- **Paul W. Beamish**, Ivey Business School, Western University, Canada
- **Derek Braddon**, Faculty of Business and Law, University of the West of England, United Kingdom
- **Paul Cashian**, Faculty of Business, Environment and Society, Coventry University, United Kingdom
- **Julia Clarke**, Leeds University Business School, United Kingdom
- **Svetlana Cicmil**, Faculty of Business and Law, University of the West of England, United Kingdom
- **Tina Dacin**, Centre for Responsible Leadership, Queen's School of Business, Canada
- **Matthew Davis**, Leeds University Business School, United Kingdom

- **Cam Donaldson**, Yunus Centre for Social Business and Health, Institutes for Applied Health Research and Society and Social Justice Research, Glasgow Caledonian University, United Kingdom
- **Barbara Dunin**, ISAE/FGV, Brazil
- **Benoit Dutilleul**, Faculty of Business and Law, University of the West of England, United Kingdom
- **ETHOS Initiative** (Commission for the Prevention of the Corruption, Court of Audit of the Republic of Slovenia, Ekvilib Institute, Energija Plus, IEDC-Bled School of Management, Siemens Slovenia, Triglav Insurance Group), Global Compact Local Network Slovenia, Slovenia
- **Norman de Paula Arruda Filho**, ISAE/FGV, Brazil
- **Patricia Flynn**, Bentley University, United States
- **Thomas Frecka**, Mendoza College of Business, University of Notre Dame, United States
- **Fabian Frenzel**, Faculty of Business and Law, University of the West of England, United Kingdom
- **Liz Frondigoun**, Glasgow Caledonian University, United Kingdom
- **Marie Koustrup Frandsen**, Copenhagen Business School (CBS), Denmark
- **Mary Gentile**, Babson College, United States
- **Yamlaksira Getachew**, Ivey Business School, Western University, Canada
- **Elizabeth Goldberg**, Babson College, United States
- **Debbie Haski-Leventhal**, Macquarie Graduate School of Management, Australia
- **Kathryn Haynes**, Newcastle University Business School, United Kingdom
- **H. David Hennessey**, Babson College, United States
- **Maya Herrera**, Asian Institute of Management (AIM), Philippines
- **Sally Hibbert**, Nottingham University Business School, United Kingdom

- **Kai Hockerts**, Copenhagen Business School (CBS), Denmark
- **K. Janardhanam Kattamanchi**, Canara Bank School of Management, Bangalore University, India
- **Diane Kellogg**, Bentley University, United States
- **Matthias Kleinhempel**, IAE Business School, Universidad Austral, Argentina
- **Oliver Laasch**, Center for Responsible Management Education (CRME), Germany and United Kingdom
- **Virginia Lasio**, ESPOL-ESPAE Graduate School of Management, Ecuador
- **Joe Lawless**, Center for Leadership and Social Responsibility, Milgard School of Business, University of Washington Tacoma, United States
- **Janette Martell**, ESADE Business School, Ramon Llull University, Spain
- **Ross McDonald**, University of Auckland Business School, New Zealand
- **Umesh Mukhi**, Audencia Nantes Schools of Management, France
- **Alan Murray**, University of Winchester Business School, United Kingdom
- **Guénola Nonet**, University Montpellier, France
- **Abiola Olukemi (Kemi) Ogunyemi**, Lagos Business School, Pan-Atlantic University, Nigeria
- **Barbara Ann Parfitt**, Glasgow Caledonian University, United Kingdom
- **Carole Parkes**, Aston Business School, United Kingdom
- **Jill Purdy**, Center for Leadership and Social Responsibility, Milgard School of Business, University of Washington Tacoma, United States
- **Andreas Rasche**, Copenhagen Business School (CBS), Denmark
- **André Sobczak**, Audencia Nantes Schools of Management, France

- **Lene Mette Sørensen**, Copenhagen Business School (CBS), Denmark
- **Agata Stachowicz-Stanusch**, The Silesian University of Technology, Poland
- **Armi Temmes**, Aalto University, School of Business, Department of Management and International Business, Finland
- **Hiro Umezu**, Keio University, Japan
- **Sarah Underwood**, Leeds University Business School, United Kingdom
- **Sandra Waddock**, Carroll School of Management, Boston College, United States
- **Alec Wersun**, Glasgow Caledonian University, United Kingdom
- **Gustavo A. Yepes Lopez**, Faculty of Business Administration, Universidad Externado de Colombia, Colombia

Index

For Product Safety Concerns and Information please contact our EU
representative GPSR@taylorandfrancis.com Taylor & Francis Verlag GmbH,
Kaufingerstraße 24, 80331 München, Germany

Printed and bound by CPI Group (UK) Ltd, Croydon, CR0 4YY

01/05/2025

01858350-0001